Getting It Right

A Call for Contextual Accuracy
and Precision in Interpreting
the Word of God

Dr. Bob Payne

Getting It Right: A Call for Contextual Accuracy and Precision in Interpreting the Word of God

© Copyright 2023 Bob Payne

ISBN: 978-1-63073-476-3
eBook ISBN: 978-1-63073-477-0

Faithful Life Publishers
North Fort Myers, FL 33903

FaithfulLifePublishers.com
info@FaithfulLifePublishers.com
888.720.0950

Published in the United States of America.
27 26 25 24 23   1 2 3 4 5

ACKNOWLDGMENTS

I am indebted to two people who have encouraged me to write. First, my late father, Jim Payne, who was a Christlike example and a wonderful Bible teacher. Second, my godly wife, Becky, who well embodies the woman of Proverbs 31.

My gratitude also goes out to my daughter who designed the book cover, and to Pastor Gary Small and Dr. Lawrence Hufhand who proofread the book and offered me their helpful comments.

TABLE OF CONTENTS

FOREWORD

Dr. Bob Payne is a God-called pastor/teacher, who is also a crusader for correct Biblical truth and understanding. His book, ***Getting it Right***, is a textbook, addressing some of the most critical issues of our day. If one is to "…*rightly divide the Word of Truth,*" one must have a comprehensive understanding of hermeneutics, which is the whole purpose of this book. It is a study guide to keep all who teach and preach the Word of God, from taking texts out of context to teach something that may or may not be true. Since we are living in a theologically confused time, I am convinced that this book will help pastors, evangelists, missionaries and Bible College students to stay true to the Scriptures and at the same time keep them from going down spurious theological paths.

Given that preachers are always looking for something new, this book, ***Getting it Right***, will also help them to stay true to the intent of the biblical writers, keeping them from teaching something that is either confusing or false. Forcing Scripture taken out of context to teach and prove a theological system is willfully being done today. This book is designed to keep this from happening.

Personally, I believe that this book could very well become one of the most valuable tools in a pastor's library, as well as an important study guide in all of our fundamental Bible colleges and Christian schools.

— Lawrence D. Hufhand, B.A., Th.M., D.Min.

INTRODUCTION

As the title of the book implies, this volume was written to emphasize the importance of handling the Word of God in a contextually accurate and precise way so that we as students of the Bible "get the meaning right." Although the book will deal with certain movements and misinterpreted passages, it is not meant to be comprehensive in scope. I could have dealt with many more passages, movements, and issues, but the ones presented here are, in my opinion, some of the more significant ones to Bible believers today.

I have noticed through the years that many professing believers have no problem with having a superficial and cursory knowledge of God's precious Book. After all, it takes less time and effort to parrot what others have said about the Bible than to actually dig out gems for themselves. In turn, shallow study breeds shallow preaching, teaching, and other presentations of the Word of God.

It is urgent that we shun laziness in interpreting the Bible, and take seriously what God has written. As we declare the Bible to others our love for God's precious Word and our love for other people should give us a real yearning for precision and accuracy and should drive us to a thorough study of the text.

We must also be reminded to approach this study with humility. If we aren't careful, a study of this sort might encourage us to snobbishly treat anyone who thinks differently about a text than we do. That attitude is sinful and unwarranted. By experience, I know that we can be diligent students of the Bible, and yet get the meaning of a passage wrong. A person may believe that he has followed all of the rules of hermeneutics properly and that his study of the text has been thorough. Then through further study, the person later discovers that he has somehow misinterpreted the passage.

This whole process of failing to understand the text correctly can be a bit discouraging. At times I have said to myself, "How could I have been so blind?!" The fact is that we all have to realize the truth that one of my professors in college used to share with the ministerial students: "We are all in different stages of ignorance." We should not let our present ignorance discourage us from pressing on in our study of God's precious Book. We are all learners and will make mistakes in interpretation from time to time. We just need to learn from those mistakes and keep pressing on toward the goal of declaring God's Word with precision and accuracy.

Throughout this work, I will be pointing out wrong approaches in Biblical interpretation and will make some strong statements concerning some misinterpreted passages. Because we all fail, my goal is not to condemn well-meaning fundamentalist brethren, nor to set myself up as the final word in hermeneutics[1] and exegesis[2]. I simply want this book to serve as a reminder to be *careful* as we approach the subject of scriptural interpretation. It is not written in formal language with the hope that every Christian reading this book can gain some insight into the interpretation of God's Word, and so assist him in ministering to others, and ultimately bring glory to our Great God.

To God be the glory!

---

1 The word may be defined as "the science and art of interpreting the Bible" (Donald K. Campbell, "Foreword," in *Basic Bible Interpretation: A Practical Guide to Discovering Biblical Truth*, ed. Craig Bubeck Sr. [Colorado Springs, CO: David C. Cook, 1991], 10.)

2 The word may be defined as "The determination of the meaning of the biblical text in its historical and literary contexts" (Donald K. Campbell, "Foreword," in *Basic Bible Interpretation: A Practical Guide to Discovering Biblical Truth*, ed. Craig Bubeck Sr. [Colorado Springs, CO: David C. Cook, 1991], 20.)

Chapter 1

THE FOUNDATION OF "GETTING IT RIGHT"

Interpretation Is Key

Have you ever noticed the many parallels between *theological* liberalism and *political* liberalism? Have you ever noticed how many who embrace theological liberalism also embrace political liberalism? Is this all just a coincidence? I don't think so. I believe that both theological liberals and political liberals in the U.S. share a common hermeneutic regarding their authoritative documents. Indeed, it's all about *interpretation*.

The political liberal interprets the U.S. Constitution as a "living document" that was written so long ago and is irrelevant to today's society. As a result, he believes that the Constitution should not be interpreted so "rigidly" (literally, or in normal language). The political liberal also believes that it is acceptable for the judiciary to "legislate from the bench." Instead of following a strict constructionist interpretation of the Constitution, it is perfectly acceptable for the courts to change or make up new laws as needed. Interpretive principles such as context and original intent are set aside as unimportant. Things outside of the Constitution, such as foreign court cases and foreign laws become influential in Constitutional interpretation. In essence, to the political liberal, the interpretation of the U.S. Constitution is reader-centered, not author-centered. Original intent is not important.

Similarly, theological liberals also treat the Word of God as a "living document" that does not need to be interpreted in a literal/normal manner. Making up doctrine, and out-right ignoring, despising, or doubting what God has clearly written in His Word is the order of the day. Many important interpretive principles such as context and an historical understanding of the text are set aside. To the theological liberal interpretation is not concerned with a meaning rising naturally *from* the text, but one that is imposed forcefully *upon* the text. In a similar manner to the political liberal, the theological liberal approaches the interpretation of the biblical text in a way that is *reader-centered* instead of *Author-centered*. To him, the original intent of the text is also irrelevant.

Although you and I may consider ourselves to be both politically and theologically "conservative," we still need to make sure that we *completely* avoid the liberal man-centered approach to biblical interpretation. We need to approach the Bible with a consistently literal hermeneutic and allow the text to speak to us. Although we may generally adhere to sound doctrine, we must not approach the text of Scripture with an inconsistent hermeneutic so as to confuse Israel and the Church, view the kingdom as something that is to be lived "here and now," or teach that the Rapture is anything but imminent. Let us strive for a biblical interpretation that allows the text to be *consistently* understood in its <u>*normal*</u> sense.

In conjunction with a Biblical hermeneutic, God has established rules of human communication that are true of *any* form of literature. Without these rules, no one could make any sense out of the Bible, much less any known piece of human literature. God gave us these rules so that He might communicate with us, and that we might know His will. Without these simple rules, the Bible becomes a confusing book of puzzles, the meaning of which is subject to the mind of man. On the other hand, when we follow these simple rules, God and His mind are restored to the central place of hermeneutics. As was stated earlier, we need an Author-centered approach to the Scriptures, not a reader-centered approach.

The Rules of a Normal Hermeneutic[1] Are Basic

In order to get Biblical interpretation right by keeping our words accurate and precise, some very basic rules need to be followed that belong to a literal/normal interpretation. As you have seen already, when we speak of interpretation, many times the word "normal" is used in place of the word "literal," "Since the word 'literal' has connotations that are easily misunderstood, labels like 'plain' or 'normal' serve more acceptably."[2] Ryrie explains why he prefers the word *normal*: "'Literal' is assumed to preclude figures of speech, etc. (which is not the case)."[3] Normal interpretation, like cream which rises naturally to the top of fresh milk, is that meaning which rises naturally (not forcefully) to the top of the text. It is the *normal* and customary way in which we as human beings communicate.

I often hear people (some of them dear friends) refer to "a dispensational hermeneutic." This is inaccurate terminology. It implies that dispensationalism is a system that has been imposed upon the Word of God. Rather, it is a filter through which we look at the Word of God. Some perhaps then look at the Bible through the filter of Covenant Theology, and others through the filter of Dispensationalism. There is obvious error here.

Instead, we need to speak of a literal/normal hermeneutic *that leads to* dispensationalism. Dispensationalism is not the *basis* of my hermeneutic. It is the *result* of the one Biblical hermeneutic. If one

---

1 I am grateful to one of my mentors, the late Dr. Clay Nuttall, for the ideas in this section. For an expansion of the ideas of which I have written, I would suggest reading a copy of Dr. Nuttall's book: Nuttall, Clay L. and Hanna, Hani. *The Normal Hermeneutic: The Only Biblical Hermeneutic*. North Fort Myers, FL: Faithful Life Publishers, 2018. Another basic book on Bible interpretation that is worthy of your time: Tan, Paul Lee. *Literal Interpretation of the Bible*. Rockville, MD: Assurance Publishers, 1978.

2 Charles Caldwell Ryrie, *Basic Theology: A Popular Systematic Guide to Understanding Biblical Truth* (Chicago, IL: Moody Press, 1999), p. 126.

3 Ibid.

approaches the scriptures with a consistently normal hermeneutic, he will by all means end up as a dispensationalist. Charles Ryrie came to this conclusion back in the 1950s: "If literal interpretation is the only valid hermeneutical principle and if it is consistently applied it will cause one to be a dispensationalist. As basic as one believes literal interpretation to be, to that extent he will of necessity become a dispensationalist."[4]

The Grammatical Rule

The Bible, like any other piece of literature, also uses *words* to communicate truth. They were written in Hebrew and Aramaic in the Old Testament, and Greek in the New Testament. Part of grammatical interpretation involves knowledge of those languages, or at least knowledge of how to use tools to access information about those languages (e.g., a Greek lexicon coded to Strong's numbering system).

Grammar is very important to those of us who believe in verbal inspiration because God didn't just inspire *concepts*, but *words*. Every word is important. Definitions and parts of speech, as well as cases, tenses, voices, and moods, are all significant. Moreover, it is also imperative to thoroughly comprehend how those words are put together (syntax) into clauses, phrases, and paragraphs.

The Historical Rule

Every piece of literature also has an historical setting. The Bible is no exception to that rule. As Dr. Paul Lee Tan wrote,

> It should be expected that between the pages of Scripture, the customs, habits, language, expressions, and sceneries of Bible lands and peoples would not remain static. The interpreter cannot afford to be sloppy in his research down the corridors of Bible times if he wants to avoid historical and cultural blunders.[5]

---

4 Charles C. Ryrie, "The Necessity of Dispensationalism," *Bibliotheca Sacra* 114 (1957): 250.

5 Paul Lee Tan, *Literal Interpretation of the Bible* (Rockville, MD: Assurance Publishers,1978), p. 32.

The farther removed we are from Biblical culture and times — and we are very far removed — the more we have to familiarize ourselves with the background behind each text. To the best of our abilities and knowledge, we need to place ourselves in the sandals of the human authors and the original readers.

The Contextual Rule

Many hermeneutics texts mention the "grammatico (or grammatical) historical method" of interpretation. Unfortunately, the contextual rule is often minimized. The truth is that *all three rules are important.* The late Dr. Clay Nuttall gives a helpful illustration in his book:

> ...the author's godly father-in-law was a dairy farmer after the old style. He was also a diligent Bible student. Dad explained quite vividly what would happen if you tried to milk a cow while sitting on a stool with one or two legs. The result would be quite messy. He explained that milking a text of the Bible requires more than one or two legs [grammatical-historical] for the same reason. Three legs [grammatical-historical-contextual] will allow the farmer to sit solidly on an uneven barn floor, while four legs would be an unstable platform, because the barn floor is uneven. While the illustration is a simple one, it is also brilliant.[6]

As is true with any other piece of literature, words and sentences should never be isolated from the rest of the literary context. Words are found in sentences, sentences are found in paragraphs, paragraphs are found in books, books are found within various parts of God's Word and in various dispensations, and both the macro and micro contexts need to be studied to render an accurate meaning for each Biblical text under consideration.

---

6 Clay L. Nuttall and Hani Hanna, *The Normal Hermeneutic: The Only Biblical Hermeneutic* (North Fort Myers, FL: Faithful Life Publishers, 2018), pp. 19-20.

When I was a student in college working on my undergraduate degree, I recall the professors "drilling" it into the heads of the ministerial students that "a text without a context is a pretext." An urgent message indeed! It bears repeating today, not just to students, but to anyone who handles the Word of God. That includes pastors, missionaries, and Bible study teachers; but does not exclude children's workers and Sunday School teachers either! Sadly, some people view accurate exegesis for children as unnecessary. The idea that since children can't comprehend what adults can, that it's therefore acceptable to spend only a few minutes in a cursory reading of the text, is being negligent of the serious responsibility that God has given to that person! James 3:1 warns the reader that teachers will incur a stricter judgment. Contextual accuracy is important for *all* ages, and there is never an excuse for a sloppy handling of the text.

It is common for believers to be critical of the cults (*and rightfully so*) when they inaccurately take scripture out of context. The problem arises when some of those same believers who claim to follow a literal/normal hermeneutic contort/distort the context of scripture to their own benefit. Some even justify their lack of contextual accuracy by saying that although they may be taking the passage out of context, the general principle behind what they are teaching is still Biblically accurate. Even if what they are teaching is broadly Biblical, it does not justify using the Word of God dishonestly to prove their point! Proper teaching from God's Word *rises naturally from the text*; it should never be forced upon the text.

Sadly, there are also those Bible teachers and preachers who are willing to sacrifice hermeneutics for homiletics. In other words, some teachers and preachers will sacrifice the accuracy of the text of scripture for "preachability." They will *purposefully* take passages out of context as long as the isolated words will prove the point(s) that they wish to make. The issue then is not "What does this passage mean," but "Will it preach?" It reminds me of the familiar humorous example of context twisting where an interpreter put the words of Matthew 27:5 together with the words of Luke 10:37, and John 13:27: "[Judas] went and hanged himself. . . Go, and do thou likewise. . . that thou doest, do quickly." God will not take lightly the actions of someone who handles His Word and purposefully twists it! Purposefully distorting the meaning of the text to prove your point is an ungodly and despicable practice.

Thankfully not all contextual problems are that devious. I believe that most of the time when there is out-of-context teaching and preaching it is *not* purposeful. Regardless, contextual inaccuracy is still a serious matter that needs to be addressed, and at its root is often the problem of careless exegesis of the passage or even a complete lack of study of the context. Other times, hard-working, well-meaning expositors will lift a passage out of its context because of "innocent" ignorance. Although we have all been guilty of this, how careful we need to be!

Paul's injunction to Timothy in 2 Tim. 2:15 is just as fresh and timely today as it was in the first century: "Study [be zealous/make every effort] to shew thyself approved unto God, a workman that needeth not to be ashamed, rightly dividing [teaching accurately] the word of truth." Taking passages out of context, even for noble reasons, should be tenaciously avoided. *The end never justifies the means!* Moreover, it destroys the credibility of our entire message and utilizes the Scripture-twisting tactic of the great Deceiver himself (Matt. 4:1-11; Lk. 4:1-8).

Precision Is Vital

As we seek the meaning of the text, not only should we follow all of the rules of a normal hermeneutic and seek contextual accuracy, but we also need to pursue *precision*. Some time ago my wife and I discussed our disdain for the modern term "ish." Lest you think I'm referring to the Hebrew word for "man," let me give you an example of how it is used in modern vernacular: "I will meet you for lunch today at "Noon-ish." "Ish" is a non-time-committal term. It completely lacks *precision*. I could meet you at 11:45 AM, 12:15 PM, or 12:30 PM and it would still be "Noon-ish."

Similarly, some sincere interpreters of the Bible develop a lack of precision toward His precious Word. The "meaning-ish" is acceptable to them. "Close enough" is satisfactory. An imprecise hermeneutic leads to an imprecise meaning, which in turn leads to imprecise obedience; something that is never acceptable to anyone who takes the Word seriously. Although there will be disagreements among sincere interpreters of God's Word, no one should ever develop a cavalier, "it-doesn't-matter-what-you-believe" attitude toward what God's Word teaches.

The bywords among "religious" people today are "openness," "tolerance," and "compromise." Most in this crowd feel that if they express *imprecision* in interpreting the Bible, it makes them more popular, and will give them a greater following for their ministries. One area that is often seen as a "minor" difference that can be handled with imprecision is baptism by immersion. Some say, it really doesn't matter if you follow immersion, effusion, or sprinkling because it's all the same thing. The question is, what commandments of the Lord do we have the option to say are "no big deal?" Does God indicate that some of His commandments are so minor that we can choose how or if we obey them? If God has given us a clear command, is it acceptable to change what He says, or at least to minimize the importance of obeying *precisely* what He says to appeal to a wider audience? To say that it doesn't matter how you baptize someone is patently not true.

In the Old Testament, *how* the Ark of the Covenant was moved was really no big thing, was it? Whether it was moved by the Levites with poles as God had commanded[7], or moved on a cart as the Philistines had done was no big deal, right? After all, it's just all methodology, and accomplishes the same thing, right? Both methods would have the same

---

7 Ex. 25:12-16: And thou shalt cast four rings of gold for it, and put *them* in the four corners thereof; and two rings *shall be* in the one side of it, and two rings in the other side of it. [13] And thou shalt make staves *of* shittim wood, and overlay them with gold. [14] And thou shalt put the staves into the rings by the sides of the ark, that the ark may be borne with them. [15] The staves shall be in the rings of the ark: they shall not be taken from it. [16] And thou shalt put into the ark the testimony which I shall give thee.

result: to move the Ark from point A to point B. Yes, *both* methods would accomplish the same result, but one method would honor the Lord by obeying His commandment, and the other one would not.

In 2 Sam. 6:1-7 and 1 Chon. 13:9-12, God was trying to teach David and Israel the vital importance of doing God's will God's way. Precision is vital when it comes to what God commands. As the Ark was being transported by cart (a method *not* prescribed by God), and everyone was celebrating before the Lord, the unthinkable happened. The oxen who were pulling the cart stumbled, and the fear was that the cart would be upset, and with it the Ark of God. Instinctively Uzzah grabbed the ark to steady it. According to the text in 2 Sam. 6:7: "God smote him there for *his* error; and there he died by the ark of God." God ended his life because of his irreverent behavior. Uzzah did not honor the holiness of God.

Someone might say, "But wait! Wasn't preventing the ark of God from falling to the ground honoring to God's holiness? Surely God wouldn't want the ark to dump onto the ground!" The problem here is that this whole incident was part of an entirely disobedient act. The ark was to be transported by the Levites with poles that fit into the sides of the ark, therefore the whole act dishonored the Lord and His holiness. Man is to obey God's will God's way. Precision in interpreting God's Word is vital!

Another example of imprecise obedience is found in Numbers 20, where Moses was told to speak to the rock so that water would gush forth from it to refresh the people and their animals. Instead, Moses struck the rock twice and water gushed out. Perhaps it was a lack of precision, but maybe God would overlook it since it resulted in the same thing. Maybe the end would justify the means. No, it wouldn't! God's judgment once again followed this disobedience, and Moses and Aaron would die before entering the Promised Land.

Lest we think that this punishment was a little harsh for such a small deviation, let's recall what God said to Moses and Aaron in Num. 20:12: "Because ye believed me not, to sanctify me in the eyes of the children of Israel, therefore ye shall not bring this congregation into the land which I have given them." God is telling them that this seemingly "small" deviation from what He commanded was the result of a lack of faith in His Word and a slighting of His holiness by Moses and Aaron in the eyes of Israel. No, this WAS a "big deal." Deciding that it wasn't that consequential to follow *exactly* what God said was a serious problem. Is it any less of a serious issue today?

Let's make sure that we take God's commandments literally and precisely as given. The truth is that such things as mode of baptism and church polity are important. To diverge from what the Bible teaches is nothing short of disobedience.

With the goals of accuracy, precision, and following a normal hermeneutic we now approach our study. As we journey through this book, we will see various movements that display a distortion of the Biblical text. In the final section of the book, we will explore some texts that are quite often twisted. May the Holy Spirit guide you, the reader, as you consider the things that are written in the rest of this work.

Chapter 2

THE LURE OF REFORMED THEOLOGY

The terms "Reformed" and "Reformed Theology" used in a negative light set some people's teeth on edge. There have been times when I have pointed out something as "Reformed Theology," and have described my hermeneutical disagreements with it, and some men have bristled at my terminology. After all, how could you disagree with the five solas[1] of the Reformation? My issue, however, is not with the "five solas," but with other teachings that have become a large part of what is commonly called "Reformed Theology."

Dr. Andy Woods makes a good point when he stresses that the Reformation focused on some wonderful doctrines that all Bible believers can support, but unfortunately, it *did not go far enough.*[2] As Dr. Woods says on the back cover of his book: "Why was the Protestant Reformation only a partial restoration? It was because they used the literal method of interpreting the Bible selectively."[3] The fact is that the Reformation did not go far enough, and as a result some Romanist doctrines still clung to the Reformers and their followers. Moreover, after the time of the Reformation, other bad doctrine also developed

---

1 *Sola scriptura* ("Scripture alone"), *sola gratia* ("grace alone"), *sola fide* ("faith alone"), *solus Christus* ("Christ alone"), *soli Deo gloria* ("glory to God alone").

2 Andy Woods, *Ever Reforming: Dispensational Theology and the Completion of the Protestant Reformation* (Taos, NM: Dispensational Publishing House, 2018). Dr. Woods' book is great, but be very careful of other things published by Dispensational Publishing House. They have a strong affinity for the writings of E. W. Bullinger, who was hyper-dispensational and a heretic.

3 Andy Woods, *Ever Reforming: Dispensational Theology and the Completion of the Protestant Reformation* (Taos, NM: Dispensational Publishing House, 2018), Back Cover.

alongside what the Reformers originally taught and became associated with other established Reformed teachings.

Because the term "Reformed" is somewhat ambiguous, some people continue to strongly object to its use. Interestingly enough, certain groups unabashedly use the term "Reformed" with no thought (e.g., "I'm/we're Reformed"), and few question what is meant. Nevertheless, because different men define the term differently in regards to a belief system, it is important to lay out what I mean by the terms, "Reformed" or "Reformed Theology," and what I believe is Biblically objectionable.

To be clear, when I use the term "Reformed Theology" I am not referring to the "five solas," but to such doctrines as strong five-point Calvinism (which supports such things as the teaching that regeneration precedes faith in Christ[4]), "Lordship salvation," covenant theology, the teaching that both the active and passive obedience of Christ join together to justify the sinner[5], the teaching that we are still under the

---

4 This was a bridge too far even for the strong Calvinist, Charles Spurgeon: If I am to preach faith in Christ to a man who is regenerated, then the man, being regenerated, is saved already, and it is an unnecessary and ridiculous thing for me to preach Christ to him, and bid him to believe in order to be saved when he is saved already, being regenerate. But you will tell me that I ought to preach it only to those who repent of their sins. Very well; but since true repentance of sin is the work of the Spirit, any man who has repentance is most certainly saved, because evangelical repentance never can exist in an unrenewed soul. Where there is repentance there is faith already, for they never can be separated. So, then, I am only to preach faith to those who have it. Absurd, indeed! Is not this waiting till the man is cured and then bringing him the medicine? This is preaching Christ to the righteous and not to sinners.

(From the sermon, "The Warrant of Faith," delivered on Sunday Morning, September 20th, 1863. Accessed online from https://archive.spurgeon.org/sermons/0531.php, March 8, 2022.)

5 David Dunlap explains this view: "Reformed theology, since the time of the Reformers, has taught that Christ provided a two-fold foundation for justification. It has been asserted that our Lord's sufferings from His birth until His death were His 'active obedience' and His sufferings and death on the cross set forth Christ's 'passive obedience.' These two aspects combine to form the basis for the believer's justification. All evangelical Christians affirm that Christ's death on the cross is the Biblical foundation for justification. However, Reformed theology insists that the obedience and sufferings of Christ prior to the cross are essential for our salvation. Calvinism affirms that the death of Christ, His 'passive obedience,' dealt with our guilt, while the merits in the

(Footnote continued on page 13)

"moral law," amillennialism, lay elders, the teaching that hell/heaven are not literal, and the playing down of dispensational distinctions which results in the misapplication of things in the gospels directly to the church. It must be kept in mind that whatever is wrong with Reformed Theology is wrong because of errant hermeneutics. Reformed Theology is really a Reformed hermeneutic that is non-literal or inconsistently literal. Here are some common hermeneutical errors followed by those who hold to Reformed theology:

The Use of an Inconsistent Hermeneutic

Examples of an inconsistent hermeneutic are numerous. In Bible prophecy, the amillennialist interprets prophecies of Christ's first coming literally (since they were undeniably fulfilled that way), and yet interprets prophecies of His second coming figuratively. The furniture and dimensions of the Old Testament tabernacle are viewed literally, but the furniture and dimensions of the Millennial Temple (Ezekiel 40-43) are viewed allegorically.

Furthermore, some who claim to hold to a normal hermeneutic and dispensationalism also dabble in Reformed Theology. They show their penchant for an inconsistent hermeneutic by not seeing dispensational distinctions in the Sermon on the Mount found in the gospel of Matthew, and so apply it directly to the church.

The Priority of Grammar and Exegesis over the Total Hermeneutical Process

Grammar, in exclusion of context and history, is often the top priority of the Reformed theologian. The exegete cannot opt for grammar and ignore the rest of the rules of a normal interpretation. Grammar is not the final arbiter concerning every question about the

---

life of Christ, his 'active obedience' provides for our justification." David Dunlap. *The Righteousness of Christ.* http://www.middletownbiblechurch.org/reformed/vicarlaw. htm (Accessed August 25, 2023). For more on this subject, see *The Dangers of Reformed Theology* at http://www.middletownbiblechurch.org/doctrine/dangerso.htm.

text. Doing a micro-analysis of a text without considering the context is folly. Ignoring historical interpretation is equally foolish.

The Dominance of Human Reasoning

Reformed Theology is viewed by some Bible expositors as an "intellectual" approach to the Scriptures. Those who do not follow a Reformed approach to the Word of God are seen as simpletons and dolts. After all, it seems so much more scholarly to spend one's time discussing the complex minutiae of the Greek or Hebrew, or to debate the meaning of what Augustine or Calvin wrote, than to find the obvious, simple meaning of a Biblical text. The fact is that those of us who don't follow Reformed theology are not in favor of "parking our brains in neutral" as we approach the Word of God. Our desire is simply to allow the text to speak for itself.

Many Reformed theologians have rejected what rises naturally from the text, and have instead opted for a "cerebral" approach as they deal with the interpretation of individual Bible texts. Much less time is spent on the text itself, and much more time is spent on logical extrapolations from the text. "What *God* thinks" is replaced with "what *I* think." A healthy debate of the meaning of a text is replaced by constant bickering over human philosophy, and the contemptuous belittling of others who do not agree with the Reformed person's "enlightened" approach. The exaltation of human reasoning in hermeneutics glorifies man and leads to arrogance.

The arrogance of those who fancy themselves as Christianity's intelligentsia commonly evidences itself in at least a few ways:

- ✓ **"We are so much more enlightened than our spiritual forefathers!"** One piece of evidence is the attitude that those given over to Reformed theology have toward the history of fundamental Christianity. They view it through a tainted lens of pride. Although every movement has those in it with wrong attitudes who act in ungodly ways, many of those following the Reformed crowd view early fundamentalists as "uneducated bumpkins" out for their self-aggrandizement. All early fundamentalists are lumped together as a bunch of men who were combative and unloving. Their "militant"[6] stand for the Word of God and biblical separation is viewed as overbearing and hateful. The newer generation's "kinder and gentler" fundamentalism embraces the kind of compromisers that early fundamentalism rejected; and, ironically, *despises* with pompous and venomous words those who desire to stand militantly for biblical truth.

✓ **"My degree from a Reformed institution is better than what you have!"** Education too has also become a major source of pride. Please do not misunderstand. I am not anti-education. I am involved in teaching in a master's degree program overseas. The problem with these individuals is not so much the *education*, but the *attitude*. Only those attaining to the level of education of these men, and at the institutions of which they approve are worthy of any serious consideration. In their opinion, an uneducated man is well-nigh worthless to the cause of Christ. Moreover, a degree from a Reformed institution is considered a badge of intellectual honor.

I wonder how a great man of God such as Harry A. Ironside would have been viewed by the Reformed crowd if he were preaching today. Although he was a godly man and a tremendous Bible teacher who pastored Moody Church from 1930 to 1948, he only had a formal education to the eighth grade. The commentaries written by this self-taught, humble servant of God are still enjoyed today by those who appreciate a literal interpretation of the text.

---

6 Dr. George Houghton does an excellent job describing biblical "militancy" in his May 1994 *Faith Pulpit* article, entitled, "The Matter of Militancy." Dr, Houghton writes, "Some, no doubt, shy away from militancy because it can easily be abused. Militancy, however, is not the same as meanspiritedness. It does not have to arise from poor motives or the desire for personal power. It does not need to be imbalanced, where 'issues' become one's hobby horse. Nor does it imply a lack of ethics - rushing into print without checking the facts, false labeling, or guilt by association. If some may be guilty of these abuses, the corrective is not an abandonment of militancy, but, rather, an ethical, careful, kind and yet firm outspokenness which stands for the truth and is willing to defend it against error. May God help us to be militant fundamentalists!"

✓ **"Never admit you don't know something."** The Reformed group seems to have a very difficult time with the words "I don't know." To them, most of the great mysteries of theology have a rational explanation. There are few mysteries when it comes to subjects such as the sovereignty of God and the responsibility of man. A doctrinal idea must be true, not so much because the biblical text says so, but because "it only makes sense." I am not suggesting that students of the Bible should not use their faculties of reasoning when studying the Word of God, but that the biblical text should *always* trump man's reasoning, even if we cannot fully comprehend all that the text implies.

An Excessive Dependence on Historical Theology in Interpretation

As I have said, the focus of Bible interpretation needs to be on the *text*. Although many things can be learned from a historical study of a text, or of a theological point in the text, the rightness or wrongness of an interpretation is not ultimately determined by who taught it or how long ago he lived. It is *not* true that if a teaching is old enough, and if the theologian teaching it is respected enough, the interpretation must be correct. Historical theology should only be a minor part of the study of Bible interpretation. It either offers support for the Biblical hermeneutic or demonstrates an allegorical hermeneutic or hermeneutical inconsistencies.

A Tendency to Read Back What Is True in the Present Dispensation into Previous Dispensations

Progressive revelation must always be considered as we study the Word of God. A failure to do so might easily lead to a misinterpretation and misapplication of the text. What is normative in our dispensation of Grace is not always normative in a former dispensation.

One example of this hermeneutical error may be found in the book by Leon Wood, *The Holy Spirit in the Old Testament*. In his work, Dr. Wood teaches that the Holy Spirit permanently indwelt Old Testament saints as He does today. Many have followed this same teaching through the years. This is a Reformed teaching since it has a tendency, to some degree, to confuse the distinction between Israel and the Church.

The plain understanding of John 14:17 teaches otherwise. Charles Ryrie was correct when he wrote,

> Obviously the Spirit of God has always been present in this world, but He has not always been a resident as one who permanently indwells the church. This was a new relationship which did not obtain even during the days of our Lord's earthly ministry, for He said to His disciples concerning the Spirit, "He dwelleth with you, and shall be in you" (John 14:17).[7]

Ryrie says more in his theology:

> The Spirit empowered Samson; later the Lord left him (Judg. 13:25; 16:20). The Spirit came on Saul and later left him (1 Sam. 10:10; 16:14). Apparently there was no guarantee of permanent presence of the Spirit in Old Testament times.[8]

John Walvoord gives a fuller explanation of John 14:17:

> It is clear that saints prior to the present dispensation had an effective ministry of the Spirit to them. This is described in John 14:17 as the fact that the Spirit "dwelleth with you." A new relationship, however, is announced, and this new relationship of the Spirit is defined as "shall be in you." Although the Holy Spirit clearly indwelt some saints in the Old Testament, this does not seem to have been universally realized and, in fact, was only bestowed sovereignly by God to accomplish His purpose in certain individuals. The Spirit being omnipresent was *with* all those who put their trust in God even if not *in*

7 Charles C. Ryrie, "The Significance of Pentecost," *Bibliotheca Sacra* 112 (1955): 331.
8 Charles Caldwell Ryrie, *Basic Theology: A Popular Systematic Guide to Understanding Biblical Truth* (Chicago, IL: Moody Press, 1999), 402.

them, and undoubtedly contributed to their spiritual life and experience. The new relationship is obviously intended to be more intimate and more effective than that which was true before the present dispensation.

Beginning on the day of Pentecost the promise of Christ, "shall be in you," was realized, and the various statements of Christ in John 14 that He would be "in you" (John 14:20) were fulfilled. The added revelation, "If any man love me, he will keep my words; and my Father will love him, and we will come unto him, and make our abode with him" (John 14:23), indicates that all three persons of the Trinity indwell the believer in the present age. This indwelling presence of God was anticipated as early as John 7:37–39 where Christ predicted that there would be rivers of living water flowing from within the believer. The explanation attached is that this refers to the Spirit "which they that believed on him were to receive."[9]

We need to be cautious and aware of the teaching of Reformed theology. Pastors need to educate their congregation about its dangers. The hermeneutic followed by those involved with it is at best inconsistently literal. Although some of its teaching is admirable and scriptural (e.g. the five solas), some of its teaching needs to be avoided because it deviates from the one Biblical hermeneutic.

The Confusion of Israel and the Church

This is particularly noticeable with those who follow a compromising position between covenant theology and dispensationalism: progressive dispensationalism. Although I will not take up the subject in detail, Ryrie does an excellent job laying out some of their puzzling beliefs that confuse Israel and the Church, in chapter 9 of his book on dispensationalism.

---

9 John F. Walvoord, "Contemporary Issues in the Doctrine of the Holy Spirit: Part II: Spiritual Renewal," *Bibliotheca Sacra* 130 (1973): 123–124.

...Progressive dispensationalism (1) teaches that Christ is already reigning in heaven on the throne of David, thus merging the church with a present phase of the already inaugurated Davidic covenant and kingdom; (2) this is based on a complementary hermeneutic that allows the New Testament to introduce changes and additions to Old Testament revelation; and (3) the overall purpose of God is Christological, holistic redemption being the focus and goal of history.[10]

The most vulnerable to this siren song of Reformed Theology seem to be young men in "full-time" ministry, or aspiring to it. Young men are attentive to the podcasts, radio programs, and books of Reformed preachers. They are drawn to their theology as a result of their winning personalities, sharp minds, and well-packaged, well-polished presentations. Beyond that, the young men are also drawn into Reformed Theology through the influence and teaching of their college and seminary professors.

If we hope to draw these young men back to a normal hermeneutic, we need to keep in mind that they are <u>not</u> going to be persuaded to abandon their love of Reformed Theology through cutesy sayings and slogans or loud verbal emphasis. Patient, consistent, thorough teaching from the Word of God is what they need. They must be confronted with the text, and encouraged to ask themselves the question: "What does the text say?"

Although it's true that some of the Reformed men have written some excellent books and preached some excellent sermons, great care needs to be taken that our recommendation of a particular book or message is not taken to be a blanket endorsement of their entire ministry. Pastors need to avoid featuring such Reformed preachers before their congregations, either in person or by constant verbal praise. The pastor may understand how to "eat the fish, and spit out the bones," but the

---

10 Charles Caldwell Ryrie, *Dispensationalism*, Rev. and expanded. (Chicago: Moody Publishers, 1995), 192.

sheep under their ministry may not. What they hear is, "My pastor likes him, so he must be OK to read/listen to."

Teachers also must be careful how they quote or present these Reformed men to their students. Students must be taught to be discerning! They must be cautioned about the errant theological tendencies of these men.

Finally, whether pastor, teacher, or student, *all of us* need to be careful about quoting these Reformed men as we teach, preach, or post on social media. Social media posts are usually short and sweet, and without sufficient explanation. You may not have understood your quote to be total approval of a Reformed individual's ministry and teaching, but others may.

Chapter 3

THE CONFUSION OF PROGRESSIVE DISPENSATIONALISM

Progressive Dispensationalism is a movement that *admittedly* has moved away from a consistently normal hermeneutic. In postmodern fashion they have combined a "complementary hermeneutic" with a normal/literal hermeneutic. They have melded dispensationalism with covenant theology and have created a monster of confusion.

In his excellent article, "Keeping Institutions True," in the July 2009 *Faith Pulpit*, Dr. Robert Delnay wrote that one of the first doctrinal shifts that institutions make is "the way that dispensationalism goes out of fashion." He goes on to say,

> It is too much to believe that a literal rapture can happen at any moment, and the teachers tend to postpone it to the remote future. The Kingdom smacks too much of "pie in the sky," and the sweet here and now becomes more urgent. **A less evident, but equally dangerous, shift is the move to progressive dispensationalism in which a school blurs the lines between Israel and the church and adopts a modified Reformed position.**[1] (Emphasis mine)

Today we are seeing on a large scale the *dangerous* slide of fundamentalist educational institutions into the Reformed hermeneutic and consequently Progressive Dispensationalism. This of course

---

1 Robert C. Delnay. "Keeping Institutions True" from the *Faith Pulpit*. July-August 2009. https://faith.edu/faith-news/keeping-institutions-true/ (Accessed September 7, 2023).

adversely affects the pastors who are the products of those institutions, and the people who sit under those pastors. Although some readers may feel that the word "dangerous," is a bit "melodramatic," Progressive Dispensationalism's threat to biblical Christianity will become apparent as we consider the movement's history, teachings, and doctrinal implications.

The Movement, the Men, and Their Message

On November 20, 1986, the "Dispensational Study Group" began meeting in connection with the annual meeting of the Evangelical Theological Society in Atlanta, Georgia. The theological discussions that took place there laid the foundation for what was labeled "progressive dispensationalism" five years later at the 1991 meeting.

In 1992 the first major work on Progressive Dispensationalism was published: *Dispensationalism, Israel and the Church*. Craig A. Blaising and Darrell L. Bock edited this work to which several well-known theologians contributed: Bruce A. Ware, Carl B. Hock, Jr., Robert L. Saucy, W. Edward Glenny, J. Lanier Burns, David K. Lowery, John A. Martin, David L. Turner, and Kenneth L. Barker. This book was quickly followed up by two other major works published in 1993: *Progressive Dispensationalism* and *The Case for Progressive Dispensationalism*.

Dr. Manfred Kober writes that the purpose of Progressive Dispensationalism seems to be…

> To develop further the system of dispensationalism. A remaking of dispensationalism to their theological presuppositions, in part adopted from European theologians. To discover similarities between dispensationalism and covenant theology. A rapprochement with a totally dissimilar system. To delineate the progressive fulfillment of God's plan in history. A rejection of God's distinctive purposes for Israel and the church. It is a sad commentary on the present situation that whereas premillennialism (out of which dispensationalism gradually emerged) arose in America primarily through early Bible

conferences held in opposition to the postmillennialism and liberalism of the day, progressive dispensationalism, in following the ecumenical spins of the times, is seeking common ground with amillennialism.[2]

The theological mantra of the Progressive Dispensational movement is "already, but not yet." Those steeped in this movement teach that Christ has ***already*** inaugurated the Davidic reign in heaven at the right hand of the Father (i.e. the throne of David), though ***not yet*** reigning as Davidic king on earth (that will occur during the millennium). Similarly, the new covenant has ***already*** been inaugurated, although its blessings are ***not yet*** fully realized (but will be in the millennium). It is obvious then that the Davidic and New Covenants are not seen as exclusively for Israel. The clear scriptural lines of demarcation between Israel and the Church are blurred by the Progressive Dispensationalist, who (as we said earlier) holds to a strange amalgamation of Covenant Theology and Dispensationalism, which in reality is an amalgamation of *hermeneutics*.

A Dangerous Movement

The bad hermeneutics of the Progressive Dispensationalist leads to an unending stream of errant theology. If the hermeneutical lens through which a person looks at the Word of God is hazy or dirty, there is always the potential for not seeing the clear teachings of Scripture accurately. Progressive dispensationalist, Craig A. Blaising, in his series, "Developing Dispensationalism," which appeared in the July – September 1988 *Bibliotheca Sacra*, admits to using a non-literal hermeneutic:

> In conclusion it can be seen that consistently literal exegesis is inadequate to describe the essential distinctive of dispensationalism. Development is taking place on how to characterize a proper hermeneutic for dispensationalists. Many do not feel, however, that the hermeneutic itself will

---

2 Manfred Kober. "The Problematic Development of Progressive Dispensationalism" (Parts 1-2) from the *Faith Pulpit*. March-April 1997. https://faith.edu/faith-news/the-problematic-development-of-progressive-dispensationalism-parts-1-2/ (Accessed September 7, 2023).

be distinctively dispensational. Furthermore dispensational interpretations of various texts are likely to modify as this development continues.[3]

As we mentioned earlier, the style of hermeneutics utilized by the Progressive Dispensationalist is termed a "complementary hermeneutic." It is an admixture of a literal and a nonliteral interpretation of the scriptures. By using this dual hermeneutic a person can say that according to the Old Testament, the Davidic Covenant was given to Israel; and that according to the New Testament, this covenant was not given to Israel alone but to the church as well. Furthermore, Christ is **already/now** reigning on the throne of David over His church in partial fulfillment of this covenant and is **not yet** reigning as He will in the Millennium.

The danger of this non-literal hermeneutic does not stop with a person's view of the biblical covenants. Once a person abandons sound interpretation, the floodgate is open to a rush of deviant doctrines. He is on the fast track toward liberalism since he is using the same hermeneutic as the liberal. David Turner's view of heaven illustrates this well. He calls a normal/literal approach to Revelation 21:21 a "hyperliteral approach." He writes concerning this passage in the book *Dispensationalism, Israel, and the Church*:

> The problem here is that the text does not speak of a 'body' of pearl material; it affirms that each gate is from one pearl. Along the same lines, the streets of gold are taken to be 'lined with' gold, but the text literally indicates that the streets are gold in their entirety. Perhaps the absence of oysters large enough to produce such pearls and the absence of sufficient gold to pave such a city (viewed as literally 1,380 miles square and high)

---

3 Craig A. Blaising, "Developing Dispensationalism Part 2 (of 2 Parts): Development of Dispensationalism by Contemporary Dispensationalists," *Bibliotheca Sacra* 145 (1988): 272.

is viewed as sufficient reason not to take these images as fully literal![4]

Additionally, the skewed hermeneutic of the Progressive Dispensationalists not only leads to a blurring of distinctions between Israel and the Church, but also an erroneous view of the Kingdom of God, which they say is the unifying theme of biblical history. Dr. Manfred Kober points out these doctrinal problems in his article, "The Problematic Development of Progressive Dispensationalism":

> By magnifying the continuity of various dispensations, revisionists are minimizing the distinctiveness of the church. Their mystery concept of the church is not that it was unrevealed in the Old Testament but it was unrealized. As a corollary, God has no separate program for the church. The church is simply a sub-category of the Kingdom. It is called a "sneak preview" of the Kingdom and a "functional outpost of God's Kingdom" (*Progressive Dispensationalism*, 257). The church is the Kingdom today. In fact, David Turner calls the church "the 'new Israel'" (Blaising and Bock, eds., *Dispensationalism, Israel and the Church*, 288). It is not surprising, therefore, that Bruce Waltke observes that Turner's "position is closer to covenant theology than to dispensationalism" (Ibid., 334). With their theological neutering of the church, the revisionists are clearly de-emphasizing the pretribulational rapture, God's distinct event involving the church.[5]

The Spirit of Compromise

In a previous quote, Dr. Manfred Kober stated that progressive dispensationalism is following "the ecumenical spins of the times" and is "seeking common ground with amillennialism." The spirit

---

4 Craig A. Blaising and Darrell L. Bach. *Dispensationalism, Israel and the Church*. (Grand Rapids: Zondervan Publishing House, 1992), 277.
5 Manfred Kober. "The Problematic Development of Progressive Dispensationalism" (Parts 1-2) from the *Faith Pulpit*. March-April 1997. https://faith.edu/faith-news/the-problematic-development-of-progressive-dispensationalism-parts-1-2/ (Accessed September 7, 2023).

that seems to motivate the Progressive Dispensationalist is that of *ecumenical compromise*. Normally to broaden one's fellowship requires one to broaden one's theology. In an effort to bring together those who hold to a normal/literal hermeneutic with those who do not, it was necessary, in Postmodern fashion, to meld together two opposite opposing ideas: Covenant Theology and Dispensationalism. Since the Progressive Dispensationalist can now play both theological sides, he is now "smart" enough to run in Reformed circles and "dialog" with Covenant Theologians, and yet he does not have to totally repudiate his dispensational roots.

The hermeneutical and theological confusion that surrounds today's Bible believer should motivate the Christian to use great caution that he uses the one Biblical hermeneutic carefully and consistently. The believer needs to stand strong and not "go with the flow" of the changing times. In a day when the loudest voices are redefining terms and calling for compromise, let's make sure that we too raise our voices in defense of what is Biblical.

Chapter 4

THE SENSATIONALISM OF "POP ESCHATOLOGY"

There is a type of prophetic preaching today that really appeals to the masses and arouses their excitement. It focuses on "signs" being fulfilled in our present day which *prove* that the rapture of the church must be **_soon_**! I call this "pop" or "popular" eschatology because generally, people love this kind of preaching, even though it is not scriptural.

Years ago J. Dwight Pentecost penned these words concerning Christ's imminent return in the air for His saints:

> Many signs were given to the nation Israel, which would precede the second advent, so that the nation might be living in expectancy when the time of His coming should draw nigh. Although Israel could not know the day nor the hour when the Lord will come, yet they can know that their redemption draweth nigh through the fulfillment of these signs. To the church no such signs were ever given. The church was told to live in the light of the imminent coming of the Lord to translate them in His presence....

> This doctrine of imminence, or "at any moment coming," is not a new doctrine with Darby, as is sometimes charged.... Such a belief in imminency marked the premillennialism of the early church fathers as well as the writers of the New Testament.[1]

1 J. Dwight Pentecost, *Things to Come* (Grand Rapids: Zondervan, 1958), pp. 202-203

Those of us who believe in a normal interpretation of the Word of God can add a hearty "amen" to the preceding words. Nevertheless, our concern is aroused as we observe some very disturbing modern trends in prophetic preaching. Many evangelists, Bible teachers, and pastors have traded in sound hermeneutics with its doctrine of imminency for an emotional, sensational, popular approach to prophetic preaching. With this style of preaching the newspaper becomes more important than the Bible, and prophetic scriptures are twisted and reshaped to fit into the mold of current events.

In this doctrinally confused generation, we need to return to a normal hermeneutic and a Bible-centered style of prophetic preaching. May those of us who are dedicated to "rightly dividing the word of truth" avoid the following perils of modern prophetic preaching:

The Peril of Prediction

Some preachers would never be bold enough to predict an exact date for the rapture of the church, but they come dangerously close. Some years ago, I read this:

> The magnetic polar reversal, predicted by computer model for 2012 is gaining more attention since its likelihood was first announced. Having moved several hundred miles across Canada the Magnetic North Pole is currently headed for Siberia. While the effects of a Magnetic Polar Reversal have never been observed by mankind, it has apparently happened in the distant past. What's unique this time is that the Sun is due for a polar reversal at the same time. I've speculated that the effects of the polar reversal could fulfill Revelation 6 and if the projected time of 2012 is correct, it fits nicely into the End Times prophecy window we opened above.[2]

---

2 Jack Kelly. "Seven Major Prophetic Signs of the Second Coming," from Rapture Ready website. https://www.raptureready.com/2011/09/16/seven-major-prophetic-signs-of-the-second-coming-by-jack-kelley/. (Accessed September 7, 2023).

No doubt, language like this is sensational and exciting, but is it biblically accurate?[3] Does it reflect a sound biblical understanding of the doctrine of Christ's imminent return?

Paul wrote to Titus: "Looking for that blessed hope, and the glorious appearing of the great God and our Saviour Jesus Christ." We see here that Paul and the saints of his day were looking for Christ's coming in the air. They believed His coming to be *at any moment*. The doctrine of imminency does not teach us that Christ <u>must</u> come in our lifetimes, or that He must come *soon* (although I pray that He does!). What it does teach us is that Christ could come at *any moment*, therefore we *always* need to be ready (1 Jn. 3:3).

The Peril of "Signs"

Those who preach the message of "pop eschatology" frequently pull passages out of context from the Olivet Discourse (which deals with the time preceding the Millennium, *not* the rapture) and distort them in such a way as to make current events fulfill them. Once again, this violates sound hermeneutics as well as the biblical doctrine of imminency. These preachers, whether knowingly or not, are distorting the meaning of the scriptures.

Some years ago, I recall a Bible teacher saying that the increase in heart disease that he saw in our country was a fulfillment of the prophecy that we see in Luke 21:26 ("men's hearts failing them for fear"), and a sign that Jesus' coming was very soon! A terrible violation of sound hermeneutics!

I also read an article on the internet several years ago by an author who used the same faulty hermeneutic. After listing various "signs" from the Olivet Discourse that "prove" that Jesus' coming must be soon, he writes in conclusion:

> As you know most of the signs in the Olivet Discourse are progressive and all are described as happening well before the

---

3 Or scientifically accurate for that matter. Remember the "prophetically significant" planet alignment of the 1980's?

end. Their main interest to us is found in the phrase "beginning of birth pangs." Natural disasters, the tendency toward war as a tool of diplomacy, famine amidst plenty (35,000 children die each day of starvation and related diseases) and pestilence are described as being common to the era but increasing in frequency and intensity as the end approaches. This was certainly the case in 2005 and is an indicator of how close we are to the end.[4]

I still wonder about one advertisement that I saw for a video about prophecy concerning Jerusalem. I'm not sure what proof text the author would use to defend this statement: "…and even see how the first moon landing fit into Bible prophecy about Jerusalem!"[5] May God help us to avoid this kind of poor theology and careless hermeneutics!

The Peril of Speculation

We live in an age where people read more novels about prophecy than they read the actual prophecy. Moreover, American Christian culture is enthralled by the speculation that they see in these novels. I see on Amazon right now that a complete set of the "Left Behind" book series consists of 16 volumes! Many of the "Left Behind" movies can be viewed over various streaming services. At one time they were even producing "Left Behind" video games, and *many* other "Left Behind" products. Although some of the "Left Behind" furor has died down, there is still a general fascination with the subject.

Some preachers of the Word of God have latched on to the speculation obsession. No longer is the Bible at the hub of their prophetic preaching. Now, speculation over who the Antichrist might be, or what part terrorism might play in prophecy takes center stage. But there are some serious dangers in prophetic speculation:

1. Speculation can violate the normal, literal sense of the biblical text.

---

4   Kelly.
5   *Perhaps Today*, pdf-formatted, web version (Sept.-Oct. 2006), p. 8

2. Some speculation gives everything in prophecy a natural explanation and so removes the supernatural element (e.g. the creatures of Rev. 9 are helicopters).

3. Some speculation partakes of urban legends (e.g. there is a computer in Europe called "the Beast").

4. An emphasis on speculation focuses on *constantly changing* current events and distracts from the exposition of the *unchanging* Word of God. Also, becoming fixated on current events leads to disappointment, discouragement, and doubt when the promise of a *soon* return (instead of an *imminent* return) does not come to pass. It also destroys the credibility of our entire message.

5. An over-emphasis on speculation leads to a preoccupation with what *might* happen than with the purpose for which a prophecy was written. This may very well lead a person to read biblical prophecy the same way that he would read a cheap science fiction novel.

Although some minor speculation concerning what a particular prophecy might be referring to is inevitable, any type of speculation must be kept in perspective. In prophetic preaching, speculation must be kept well in the background; the Word must be at the forefront. Moreover, speculation is man-centered. It must not be given authority on par with the Word of God.

Our Focus

Prophetic preaching and teaching must remain focused on a normal interpretation of the Word of God, and the any-moment return of the Lord Jesus Christ for His Church. Those who handle the Word of God must be cautious not to predict the time of the coming of Christ, nor twist the scriptures in an effort to show that His coming is near. Furthermore, teachers and preachers must be extremely careful not to over-emphasize prophetic speculation. In this day of doctrinal drift and sensationalism, prophetic preaching must be anchored in the unchanging Word of God.

Chapter 5

THE ERRONEOUS TEACHING CONCERNING THE JUDGMENT SEAT OF CHRIST

Those who follow a normal, natural meaning of the Biblical text believe that a judgment of believers takes place in heaven following the rapture of the church (2 Cor. 5:10). Every church-age believer will stand before the Judgment Seat (Gk. *bema*) of Christ to be evaluated by our Lord. With this, most who believe in a pre-tribulational rapture would agree. The disagreement among pre-tribulationalists has less to do with *where* and *when* the *Bema* judgment will take place and more to do with the *character* of the judgment.

Some believe that the *Bema* is an *evaluation of sin* where Christians will be punished, or at least publicly humiliated for unconfessed sins. Others believe that the *Bema* is *an evaluation of the nature of a believer's works* (whether good or worthless). The disagreement between these two sides is significant since it involves a person's view of the very nature of the atonement. So, what saith the Scripture?

Is the Believer Saved from Sin, or Not?

The Bible is plain concerning what happens the moment a person receives Jesus Christ as Savior. His sins—past, present, and future— are all forgiven because of the blood of Christ (Col. 2:13). No longer does he stand before Him as a condemned sinner. The believer's sin was charged to Christ's account, and He paid for it (2 Cor. 5:19, 21).

The righteousness of Christ is charged to the believer's account (1 Cor. 1:30; 2 Cor. 5:21). As a result of the believing sinner's new standing, God is able to judicially declare him to be righteous (justification), and none dare bring a charge against him (Rom. 8:33)! The late J. Dwight Pentecost mentions how unbiblical it is to say that we will be held accountable for unconfessed sins at the *Bema*:

> This presupposes the fact that my sins have not been completely and perfectly dealt with by the blood of Christ. It presupposes that God is keeping a record of all my iniquities so that He can present them before me when I stand in His presence. Such is contrary to the holiness of God and to the finished work of the Lord Jesus Christ.[1]

Heb. 10:14, 17-18 states, "For by one offering he hath perfected forever them that are sanctified....And their sins and iniquities will I remember no more. Now where remission of these is, there is no more offering for sin." The Christian's sins have been atoned for completely and forever. Nothing more needs to be done: "there is no more offering for sin." The believer's sins will no longer be brought up against him, nor does he have to do anything to "re-atone" for them (not now, at the *Bema*, or in eternity).

Is the Believer Held Accountable at the *Bema* for Unconfessed Sin?

The purpose of the believer confessing his sins as taught in 1 John 1:9 is not to keep himself "saved." As Charles Ryrie wrote, "Our family relationship is kept right by His death; our family fellowship is restored by our confession."[2] Samuel L. Hoyt expands these thoughts in the second of his excellent two-part article on the Judgment Seat of Christ:

---

1 J. Dwight Pentecost, *Prophecy for Today: An Exposition of Major Themes on Prophecy* (Grand Rapids: Zondervan Publishing House, 1961), p. 153, as cited in Samuel L. Hoyt, "The Judgment Seat of Christ in Theological Perspective Part 1: The Judgment Seat of Christ and Unconfessed Sins," *Bibliotheca Sacra* 137 (1980): 36.

2 Charles Caldwell Ryrie, *A Survey of Bible Doctrine* (Chicago: Moody Press, 1972).

Another argument which supports the position that the Christian's sins will not be an issue at the βῆμα relates to the present effect of unconfessed sins. Unconfessed sins relate to fellowship in *this* life. Any unconfessed sin stands as a barrier to fellowship and growth in one's present relationship to God. Confession brings immediate forgiveness and restoration of fellowship between the Christian and God. This is present-tense forgiveness and deals with "family" forgiveness. For example, 1 John is a "family" epistle addressed to the "born ones" or to τεκνία μου ("my little children"). First John 1:9 refers to "family," experiential forgiveness: "If we confess our sins, he is faithful and just to forgive us our sins, and to cleanse us from all unrighteousness."

The daily forgiveness of those who are within the family of God is distinguished from judicial and positional forgiveness which was applied forensically to all of a person's sins the moment he believed in the Lord Jesus Christ. Paul writes of this forensic forgiveness in Colossians 2:13: "And you, being dead in your sins and the uncircumcision of your flesh, hath he quickened together with him, *having forgiven you all trespasses*." The point Paul makes is that *the believer is completely forgiven legally before the sin is even committed.* The question that arises concerning a believer's sins is between the Father and a son, and not between a judge and a criminal. The legal side has already been settled. The question revolves around a contemporaneous relationship between the Father and a son. If there is a barrier which arises through a son offending his Father, there must be family forgiveness. It is not forensic forgiveness for that has been eternally granted and efficaciously applied the moment he became a son.[3]

The Scripture is clear. The purpose of regular confession is the maintenance of family fellowship in this life. The penalty for

---

3 Samuel L. Hoyt, "The Judgment Seat of Christ in Theological Perspective Part 1: The Judgment Seat of Christ and Unconfessed Sins," *Bibliotheca Sacra* 137 (1980): 37–38.

unconfessed sin is not humiliation at the *Bema* of Christ, but loss of intimate fellowship right now.

The Purpose of the *Bema*

The teaching of the Word of God is clear that the judgment seat of Christ is not for the purpose of bringing up the past sins of the believer in order to punish the Christian in some way (2 Cor. 5:10). The Judgment Seat is basically a *reward* seat. The *Bema* in the context of 2 Cor. 5:10 refers to the umpire's stand at the Isthmian games. During those games the contestants would compete for the prize while the judges carefully scrutinized the contestants to make sure that the rules of the game were followed. The person who followed the rules and won a particular event was led by the judge to the *bema*. At the judgment seat he was crowned with a laurel wreath as a symbol of victory (1 Cor. 9:24-25).

At the *Bema* of Christ, the *quality* of each man's work will be tried. Faithful stewards will be rewarded and unfaithful ones will experience loss of rewards (1 Cor. 3:10-15; 1 Cor. 4:2). According to 2 Cor. 5:10, all those who have trusted in Christ as Savior will *appear* before Christ. The Greek word behind the translation *appear* is much stronger than the English might suggest. The idea here is of *being made manifest.* The word refers to more than just our presence. It is a revelation of *who we really are.* Attitudes and motives will be apparent at the *Bema,* as well as good qualities concerning our works that may have been misunderstood by others. The verse goes on to mention "the things done in [our] body." Once again, this demonstrates that this judgment is an examination of our works, whether they are good or worthless/substandard.

The Results of the *Bema*

Some have compared the Judgment Seat of Christ to a commencement. Everyone graduating is overjoyed to be moving on to new horizons. Some who are graduating have put forth real effort, utilizing whatever mental abilities that they have been given, and graduate with a great amount of satisfaction and reward for their labors. Others, who were not diligent students, will have a certain amount of disappointment and regret knowing that they could have done better in their academic careers. Overall, the emotion at a commencement is joy, not sorrow. Samuel Hoyt brings biblical balance to the subject when he writes, "To overdo the sorrow aspect of the judgment seat of Christ is to make heaven hell. To underdo the sorrow aspect is to make faithfulness inconsequential."[4]

Those who were not faithful stewards of what God had given to them will suffer loss at the judgment seat (1 Cor. 3:15; 1 Cor. 9:24-27). Some will have lived so unfaithfully that, when their Lord appears, they will "be ashamed before him" (1 John 2:28). Varying degrees of reward will also be featured at the *Bema* (1 Cor. 3:12, 14). The Scriptures tell us in 1 Cor. 4:5 that Christ will "both bring to light the hidden things of darkness, and will make manifest the counsels of the hearts," and that "every man [will] have praise of God." Although we can be assured that the rewards of faithful service are incredible, we know very little about what form these rewards will take. The Bible portrays some of these rewards as crowns (which will be cast at the feet of Christ), yet the specifics are not mentioned.

The Effects of the *Bema* upon the Believer

Christ's coming is imminent. He could come at any moment to snatch us up to heaven. We could be standing very soon before our Lord at the Judgment Seat. Although our faithful service for Christ in this life may have gone unnoticed, or may have been misunderstood and mischaracterized, the Lord knows our hearts and will reward us fairly. We can be encouraged to know that "God is not unjust so as to forget your work and the love which you have shown toward His name" (Heb. 6:10).

Additionally, not only should the believer be encouraged, but he needs to make sure that he is ready for the Judgment Seat by remaining pure and being faithful to what the Lord has entrusted us: "every man that hath this hope in him purifieth himself, even as he is pure" (1

4 Samuel L. Hoyt, "The Judgment Seat of Christ in Theological Perspective Part 2: The Negative Aspects of the Christian's Judgment," *Bibliotheca Sacra* 137 (1980): 131.

John 3:3). We need to make sure that we are being faithful with all of the things over which God has made us stewards, including time, talents, spiritual gifts, money, possessions, as well as the gospel message. We need to heed the warning of the apostle John in 2 John 8: "Look to yourselves, that we lose not those things which we have wrought, but that we receive a full reward." Faithfulness will be rewarded and unfaithfulness will result in loss of rewards. We need to keep our eyes on the eternal, not on the temporal: "For which cause, we faint not; but though our outward man perish, yet the inward man is renewed day by day. For our light affliction, which is but for a moment, worketh for us a far more exceeding and eternal weight of glory; while we look not at the things which are seen, but at the things which are not seen: for the things which are seen are temporal; but the things which are not seen are eternal" (2 Cor. 4:16-18).

Chapter 6

TWISTED OLD TESTAMENT TEXTS

"Touch not mine anointed, and do my prophets no harm."
1 Chron. 16:22; Ps. 105:15

Since I began to pastor, I have been extremely concerned not only with the misuse of these two passages, but the unbiblical teaching and attitude concerning pastoral ministry that goes along with them. In the case of 1 Chron. 16:22 and Ps. 105:15, both interpretive and doctrinal errors go hand-in-hand. "Touch not mine anointed, and do my prophets no harm" is usually erroneously applied in this way: "Since the pastor is God's anointed man and God's prophet, no one has any right to question a pastor as to his morals, ethics, or teachings. God plainly tells us in His Word to 'touch not mine anointed.' All discipline of 'God's man' should be left to God Himself."

Roy Branson, Jr. reflects this unbiblical view in his book, *Dear Preacher, Please Quit!*:

We're saying that if a man of God is out of the will of God, leave him to God to take care of; and believe it, God will take care of him. One may say, "Well, what if he's tearing up our church?" Either live with it or go to another church, but don't ever try to get rid of the preacher. You may be right and the preacher may be wrong, but, if he's called of the Lord, that's God's man and we will tell you God will take care of him.

When you try to do it, you put yourself in the position of Saul's Amalekite.[1]

At the end of the chapter Dr. Branson gives an illustration of a young lady who approached him following a service. She said that she was having an affair with a well-known local pastor. Roy Branson ends his story (and chapter) with these disturbing words:

> What did the author do? He prayed with the young woman and she sought and received God's forgiveness. He told no one, not even his wife, about the problem. Leave God's man to God to straighten out.

> By the way, the above affair was ended because the young lady got right with God and refused to continue it. [Nothing is said of the pastor's repentance or his resignation.]

> Finally, let us be sure we understand that God put no qualifications, no "unless" or "if" on the warning, "Touch not mine anointed and do my prophets no harm."[2]

As I stated before, I believe that the position articulated above abounds in both contextual and doctrinal error:

Contextual Error

If we are to set these passages in their proper context, two questions need to be answered: 1) To whom do "mine anointed" and "my prophets" refer? and, 2) What does it mean to "touch" them or "harm" them? The contexts of our passages make the answers to these questions plain (both contexts are very similar[3]). Notice whom God is addressing in Psalm 105:6-15:

---

1 Roy L. Branson, Jr., *Dear Preacher, Please Quit!* (Kingsport, TN: The Kingsport Press, 1987), pp. 33-34.

2 Ibid.

3 Why are they similar? Eugene Merrill gives us the reason as he comments on the 1 Chronicles passage: "David then must have excerpted parts from his earlier poetry and woven them together into this beautiful piece. Eugene H. Merrill, "1 Chronicles," in *The Bible Knowledge Commentary: An Exposition of the Scriptures*, ed. J. F. Walvoord and R. B. Zuck, vol. 1 (Wheaton, IL: Victor Books, 1985), 607.

[6] O ye seed of Abraham his servant, ye children of Jacob his chosen. [7] He *is* the LORD our God: his judgments *are* in all the earth. [8] He hath remembered his covenant for ever, the word *which* he commanded to a thousand generations. [9] Which *covenant* he made with Abraham, and his oath unto Isaac; [10] And confirmed the same unto Jacob for a law, *and* to Israel *for* an everlasting covenant: [11] Saying, Unto thee will I give the land of Canaan, the lot of your inheritance: [12] When they were *but* a few men in number; yea, very few, and strangers in it. [13] When they went from one nation to another, from *one* kingdom to another people; [14] He suffered no man to do them wrong: yea, he reproved kings for their sakes; [15] *Saying*, Touch not mine anointed, and do my prophets no harm.

It is clear from vv. 9-12 that the "anointed" and "prophets" of v. 15 are a reference to Abraham, Isaac, Jacob, and their descendants. Israel is being addressed. Moreover, it is apparent from vv. 13-14 that "touching" them, or "harming" them refers to protection from physical danger. J. Barton Payne's comments on 1 Chronicles 16:18-22 shed light on why God used the terms "anointed" and "prophets:"

> The titles by which the patriarchs are described possess, at this early period, more generalized meanings than those they came to have later. They are called "anointed"…, in the sense of being set apart by God's Spirit--a phrase elsewhere used specifically for prophets (1 Kings 19:16), priests (Exod 29:7), and kings (1 Sam 2:35), with whom the presence of the Spirit was symbolized by a visible anointing with oil, and ultimately for Jesus (Christ = Messiah = "anointed"; 1 Sam 2:10; Ps 2:2; Acts 10:38).
>
> The patriarchs are also called "prophets," in the sense of being recipients of God's special revelation--a title later used specifically for those who proclaimed God's revealed will …. Abraham was thus designated a "prophet," at the time of God's special protection against Abimelech, the Philistine king of

Gerar (Gen 20:7); others of the patriarchs did, however, make specific predictions (e.g., Jacob, Gen 48:19; 49:1).[4]

To apply this passage to the modern pastor is inaccurate and a misuse of the Word of God. The reference is clearly to Israel, not to an officer in the local church. Moreover, the local church was yet a mystery that was not to be revealed until the dispensation of grace. The fact is, those who erroneously apply these texts to the shepherd of a local church are applying it to the wrong people and in the wrong dispensation.

Additionally, keep in mind that Ps. 105:15 contains "the warning the Lord gave to the kings in v. 14,[5]" not people in general. It is also interesting to note that the phrase "touch not mine anointed" is telling the kings more than just "Don't say anything negative or accusatory about my people." This would be Branson's primary application. As the text demonstrates, the primary reference of "touch not" and "do no harm" is persecution and physical harm of God's covenant people.

Doctrinal Error

There are some erroneous doctrinal implications behind these two twisted texts. As we have said those who hold that Ps. 105:15, and 1 Chon. 16:22 may be applied to pastors of local churches also believe that the pastor is sovereign in the local church, and no one has the right to question anything he says or does.

Is this true? What saith the Scriptures?

Feed [Shepherd] the flock of God which is among you, taking the oversight *thereof*, not by constraint, but willingly; not for filthy lucre, but of a ready mind; [3] Neither as being lords over *God's* heritage, but being ensamples to the flock. [4] And when the chief Shepherd shall appear, ye shall receive a crown of glory that fadeth not away. (1 Peter 5:2-4)

---

4 J. Barton Payne, "1 Chronicles," in *The Expositor's Bible Commentary*, gen. ed. Frank E. Gaebelein, vol. 4 (Grand Rapids: Zondervan Publishing House, 1988), p. 391.

5 Daniel J. Estes, *Psalms 73–150*, ed. E. Ray. Clendenen, vol. 13, New American Commentary (Nashville, TN: B&H Publishing Group, 2019), p. 287.

Does this text describe the shepherd as the sovereign ruler of the local church whose dictates can never, ever be questioned? Hardly. Yes, the pastor is the leader (1 Tim. 5:17: "rule") and "bishop" or "overseer" of the entire ministry of the local church. However, that does not mean that his actions should never be questioned. Paul lays out the proper procedure for rebuking an elder/pastor in 1 Tim. 5:19-20: "Against an elder receive not an accusation, but before two or three witnesses. Them that sin rebuke before all, that others also may fear." The pastor as a member of the local church is subject to discipline in the same way as any other member. Robert Gromacki wrote about v. 19: "As members of a church, elders are not immune to the procedure of discipline. The same standards apply to them as well as to the laymen[6]."[7] Furthermore, some sins of the pastor may disqualify him permanently from the ministry of shepherd.

Some view the pastor as "clergy" which places the pastor on a higher, more exalted level than his people (the "laity). The Bible knows nothing of this unbiblical, man-made distinction between "clergy" and "laity." Our Lord taught us that ministry is not something executed from a lofty position above others, but it is something performed from the "low" position of Christ-like humility (Matt. 20:26-28) as the Lord's servant.

1 Peter 5:2-4 which was mentioned before is instructive. Peter does not tell us that the pastor is a monarch, a king, or a dictator. He uses the term "shepherd" in v. 2. Peter continues in v. 3 to instruct his readers that a shepherd should not be a man who "lords it over" (*katakurieuo*: "exercising dominion for one's own advantage"[8]) his sheep, but instead, he should be an example to the flock. Clearly, the scriptures indicate to us that the pastor is not to be a dictator, but one who leads by example.

---

6 Although I dislike the term "layman," we understand Dr. Gromacki's meaning.
7 Robert Gromacki, *Stand True to the Charge: An Exposition of I Timothy*, The Gromacki Expository Series (The Woodlands, TX: Kress Christian Publications, 2002), p. 146.
8 Timothy Friberg, Barbara Friberg, and Neva F. Miller, *Analytical Lexicon to the Greek New Testament*, Baker's Greek New Testament Library (Grand Rapids: Baker, 2000), Entry 15145, κατακυριεύω; BibleWorks, v. 10.

Although the pastor is to lead by example, we need to keep a Biblically balanced view of the pastoral ministry. We shouldn't over-emphasize the "leading by example" aspect of the pastorate. By doing so, some have weakened the office of the pastor, and have relegated the shepherd to a hired hand of the flock who does as he is told. This too is a distorted view of the ministry. Once again, the Word of God provides clear guidance in this area:

> This *is* a true saying, If a man desire the office of a <u>bishop</u> <u>[overseer]</u>, he desireth a good work. (1 Tim. 3:1)

> Let the elders that <u>rule [administration, or presiding over the</u> <u>affairs of the local church]</u> well be counted worthy of double honour, especially they who labour in the word and doctrine. (1 Tim. 5:17)

> <u>Obey</u> them that have the <u>rule over you ["leaders"]</u>, and <u>submit</u> <u>yourselves</u>: for they watch for your souls, as they that must give account, that they may do it with joy, and not with grief: for that *is* unprofitable for you. (Heb. 13:17)

According to the previous scriptures the pastor rules and presides over the entire ministry of the local church (both the "spiritual" and "material"). Although his position demands respect, submission, and obedience, he is still not the dictator and king of the local church. BALANCE is extremely important in this area! Dr. Clay Nuttall brings some needed clarity to this issue:

> A real danger also exists in not seeing his [the pastor's] administration in balance....It has been soundly preached that a bishop's administration and rule are by example and precept. That is true. Woe to the pastor who does not preach the Word. It alone is the final Authority and Guidebook. Shame on the pastor who lords it over God's heritage. Let us all deride dictatorial self-centeredness....

> Let not man say, however, that the pastor's leadership is limited to his influence and example, or to the simple leadership of

43

teaching as verbalization and integration into his own actions and the actions of others. To take from him responsibility and authority, to enforce, by rule, Bible commands in the local church is not an attack on him but on Christ.

The Lord Himself imposed that oversight (1 Pet. 5:1-4) and the pastor will answer directly to the Chief Shepherd for exercise of it. The bishop is to be obeyed (Heb. 13:7, 17) and that implies much more than being an example. He is to rule (1 Tim. 5:17) and anything less than that is a failure. Some have played grammatical games and contextual shuffling to deny the Lord's instruction to undershepherds. Those actions are beneath the dignity of the office.[9]

Pastoral ministry is like a husband-wife relationship. The husband is the loving leader of the home; the pastor is the loving leader of the local church. The husband is not the dictator in his home; neither is the pastor the dictator of the local church. The husband's leadership does not mean that his wife is just to "shut up" and never question *anything* that he does. The same is true of the pastor and "flock." The shepherd is not the absolute monarch of the local church who should never be questioned. He is the overseer of the ministry. The old nature, full of pride and arrogance, desperately wants to justify a dictatorial leadership style. The carnal man finds comfort in the statement: "God says never to question anything that I ever do or say." May God help us to find a biblical balance in our view of the pastor's leadership in the local church.

"If my people, which are called by my name, shall humble themselves, and pray, and seek my face, and turn from their wicked ways; then will I hear from heaven, and will forgive their sin, and will heal their land." 2 Chron. 7:14

I have observed that this passage is quoted by everyone from religious politicians, to pastors and evangelists. The passage is applied

9 Clayton L. Nuttall, *The Weeping Church: Confronting the Crisis of Church Polity* (Schaumburg, IL: Regular Baptist Press, 1985), pp. 103-104.

directly to appeal to personal and national revival. After the passage is quoted, something similar to the following is said,

> "We Christians are God's people and called by His Name. We need to do as the scripture says by humbling ourselves, praying, seeking God's face, and turning from our wicked ways. This is God's formula for revival and our country's survival. If we do what is written here and turn back to Him, God promises that He will forgive our sin and heal our country."

No doubt there is some truth in what I just wrote. It's an appealing message! After all, who would disagree with the fact that the U.S. has grievous national sins for which it needs to repent? Even though all who take the Word of God seriously would agree with some of the truths presented in the previous statement, 2 Chron. 7:14 still needs to be approached with great caution to consistently utilize the one Biblical hermeneutic. There are subtle dangers in the interpretation and application of this text that need to be avoided.

Remember that in hermeneutics that there is first observation of the text, then interpretation, and then finally application. We cannot skip the step of *interpretation* no matter how "powerful" we believe the *application* to be.[10] A good practitioner of the science and art of hermeneutics will learn how to ask good questions of the text and allow the text to speak for itself. Some questions that need to be honestly answered of this text are…

Under What Dispensation Was This Promise Given?

Keep in mind that this was given under the dispensation of the Law. That in itself should shoot up a bright red flag concerning the common interpretation of this text. Remember that God progressively revealed His will to man through the ages. Under each successive dispensation a group of people, a nation, or mankind in general was given new revelation, and a responsibility to obey. Each dispensation

---

10 See chapter one, "The What and Why of Bible Interpretation" of Roy B. Zuck's book, *Basic Bible Interpretation: A Practical Guide to Discovering Biblical Truth*, ed. Craig Bubeck Sr. (Colorado Springs, CO: David C. Cook, 1991).

concludes with a failure to obey resulting in judgment. Showers reminds his readers that under the Law:

> The special revelation which God gave to Israel for the fifth dispensation is recorded in Exodus 20-Deuteronomy. It consisted of the Mosaic Law with its 613 commandments. These gave in detail God's will for the moral, civil, and ceremonial aspects of Israel's life.[11]

Who are "My people?" To Whom Is the Promise Addressed?

The context is clear in vv. 11-14. *Israel* is "My people" and the promise is addressed to *them*. This is not a promise that can be claimed by the church or modern believers.

What is the Historical Context of This Passage?

Charles Ryrie lays out the context directly and simply: "The clear context of the promise relates to the dedication of Solomon's temple in Jerusalem. After Solomon's magnificent prayer and the offering of the multitude of sacrifices, God appeared to Solomon at night and reiterated the necessity of walking with God and punishment if he did not do so."[12]

What Is Being Promised?

So many neglect the context of 2 Chron. 7:14. When we read verses 13-14 together, the promise becomes obvious: "If I shut up heaven that there be no rain, or if I command the locusts to devour the land, or if I send pestilence among my people; If my people, which are called by my name, shall humble themselves, and pray, and seek my face, and turn from their wicked ways; then will I hear from heaven,

---

11 Renald E. Showers, *There Really Is a Difference!: A Comparison of Covenant and Dispensational Theology* (Bellmawr, NJ: FOI Gospel Ministry, Inc., 1990), p. 42.

12 Charles Ryrie, *Ryrie's Practical Guide to Communicating Bible Doctrine* (Nashville, TN: Broadman & Holman Publishers, 2005), p. 64.

and will forgive their sin, and will heal their land." Recall Deuteronomy 27-29 where the blessings and the curses of the Mosaic Covenant are given. Disobedience to the Mosaic Covenant would result in the curses mentioned in Deuteronomy, and obedience would result in the blessings recorded there. If God's people sinned, things such as drought, locust, and plague would curse the land, BUT if Israel repented, restoration to the covenant relationship would be granted and the land would be "healed" of the curses mentioned in v. 13. We know that eventually both Israel and Judah would suffer captivity because of their disobedience and idolatry. Deuteronomy 30:1-5 mentions Israel's final future restoration after the blessing and the curse have been fulfilled (v. 1) and they will ultimately become an obedient people.

How Is This to Be Applied Today?

Once again, Ryrie's comments are excellent here, and draw together everything that we have said so far:

> While one may use verse 14 as a general principle of the requirements for blessing being humility, prayer, devotion, and repentance, the specific blessing promised in this verse is the healing of the land of Israel when "My people"—that is, Israel—repents. To stretch this promise to assure blessing on any nation whose citizens repent is simply that—a stretch, though admittedly an appealing one. Too often this verse serves as a call to God's people (Christians) to repent in order to heal (that is, preserve) our land (America). As far as I can discern, there is no promise in the Bible that America will be preserved even if the population were 100 percent believers. To be sure, this verse contains an important principle: repentance on the part of God's people brings individual blessing, but it does not contain a promise that the blessing will extend to the nation of those people. An individual and specific promise has undergone a metamorphosis into a general principle supposedly applicable to many other nations. It would be

better to use Proverbs 14:34: "Righteousness exalts a nation, but sin is a disgrace to any people."[13]

So, although applications can be made from 2 Chron. 7:14 we should never directly apply the promises made here to Israel to the Church (the Church and Israel are distinct), or to our country (we are not Israel). The promise was made to the nation of Israel under the dispensation of the Law after the dedication of Solomon's temple. It concerns their disobedience to the Mosaic Covenant and potential repentance that would restore them to an intimate relationship with God. That repentance would also reverse the curses mentioned in v. 13 and heal the land of Israel. This call to repentance is no different than the message of many of the Old Testament prophets.

"He brought me up also out of an horrible pit, out of the miry clay, and set my feet upon a rock, and established my goings." Ps. 40:2

This is a popular text that is often preached as a passage that describes the sad state of a lost person ("horrible pit...miry clay") who has come to know God. The preacher would go on to say that God has pulled him out of the horrible pit of sin and judgment and has saved him from sin and has given him a new life ("set my feet upon a rock, and established my goings"). Even though this text may "preach well" using that meaning, and the meaning may match the general teaching of the Word of God concerning the doctrine of salvation, the question we need to answer is, "Using sound hermeneutics, can we say based on the context and the historical situation that the psalmist is talking about spiritual salvation?" The psalmist (David, according to the inscription) definitely speaks of some type of deliverance here, but to what type of "salvation" is he referring?

Allen Ross presents the thrust of this passage quite well:

> The psalm begins with David's joyful report to the congregation about his deliverance and an encouragement to them to trust the Lord. **God** did something wonderful for him after a long

---

13 Ibid., pp. 64–65.

period of prayerful, patient waiting. Using figurative language to describe his distress and release, he affirmed that **the LORD** saved him from his dilemma (like being in a **slimy pit** with **mud and mire**) and established him firmly **on a rock**.[14]

Peter Craigie also comments on the passage:

The psalm begins with a general thanksgiving for past acts of divine deliverance; by this introductory act of thanksgiving, the king establishes the ground of precedent, framed in the appropriate praise, by which he will move forward to a prayer for further deliverance in a new crisis that threatens his life and kingdom. Just as past prayers had been answered after patient waiting (v 2), so too would his present prayer.

The language of v 3 ("the pit of desolation," the "slimy mud") is indicative of a former occasion in which God had saved the suppliant's life. Although it is possible that the former deliverance was from severe sickness (cf. Ps 30:3–4), the royal context of this psalm makes it more likely that the deliverance was experienced in a military crisis. Near disaster and death were turned into victory and stability (v 3b)....[15]

The context supports Ross's and Craigie's comments. Notice vv. 13-17 of the psalm:

Be pleased, O LORD, to deliver me: O LORD, make haste to help me. [14] Let them be ashamed and confounded together that seek after my soul to destroy it; let them be driven backward and put to shame that wish me evil. [15] Let them be desolate for a reward of their shame that say unto me, Aha, aha. [16] Let all those that seek thee rejoice and be glad in thee: let such as love thy salvation say continually, The LORD be magnified. [17] But

---

14 Allen P. Ross, "Psalms," in *The Bible Knowledge Commentary: An Exposition of the Scriptures*, ed. J. F. Walvoord and R. B. Zuck, vol. 1 (Wheaton, IL: Victor Books, 1985), 824.

15 Peter C. Craigie, *Psalms 1–50*, vol. 19, Word Biblical Commentary (Dallas: Word, Incorporated, 1983), 314–315.

I *am* poor and needy; *yet* the Lord thinketh upon me: thou *art* my help and my deliverer; make no tarrying, O my God.

It is clear, especially when we read v. 14, that David is referring to *temporal* salvation/deliverance, and not spiritual salvation/deliverance. David was in danger. There were those who sought after his "soul (life) to destroy it." They wished him evil. At the beginning of the psalm, we see that David takes heart during this new crisis, recalling that God had saved him from a past temporal crisis.

A careless use of hermeneutics interprets this passage as a testimony of David's spiritual salvation from sin. The context clearly demonstrates that the deliverance here is David's deliverance from the danger and threats of his enemies. The danger is pictured by the pit of miry clay, which is similar to the cistern into which Jeremiah was thrown (Jer. 38:6). David is stuck in the muck and mire of a seemingly hopeless situation, but God brings deliverance from it! This is symbolized by lifting him out of this cistern and setting his feet, not in muck and mire, but on a rock, making his footsteps firm.

"And he hath put a new song in my mouth, even praise unto our God: many shall see it, and fear, and shall trust in the LORD." Ps. 40:3

Please keep in mind the exegesis from the last section. David's deliverance from a desperate situation (vv. 1-2) sets up the context for v. 3. As Ross wrote, "This deliverance gave him **a new song** for rejoicing (cf. 33:3; 96:1; 98:1; 144:9; 149:1)."[16]

Often this passage, and others like it, are used to demonstrate how important proper music standards are, and how worldly music needs to be rejected by the Christian. Those who believe in exegeting the passage in this way elaborate that we need to forsake the music of the old life and sing a "new song" that matches our new spiritual state as a believer. Although I completely agree that worldly music ought to be rejected and replaced by godly music, and I teach very similar things from other

---

16 Ross, p. 824.

passages in the Word of God,[17] is David teaching that *here*? Could it be that some well-intentioned people are using the wrong passage to teach the right thing?

This is really a simple matter. Ask the text the question, and you will find your answer. Question: "Was David saying that at one time he was an unbeliever and used to listen to and play sensual, ungodly music; and now, since he is a believer and has a new life, he listens to and plays a godly "new song?" The answer is obvious. First of all, in this verse, David is not presenting his standard of music. Second, in the text David is not referring to a change in music from the sinful past to the righteous present. He is clearly saying that the temporal deliverance/salvation mentioned in vv. 1-2, "afforded him new matter for thanksgiving (cf. 33:3), and became in his mouth 'praise to our God;' for the deliverance of the chosen king is an act of the God of Israel on behalf of His chosen people."[18] This "new song" "is so called because God makes the psalmist's situation new by his intervention.[19]" As a result of all of this, "many shall see *it*, and fear, and shall trust in the LORD" (v. 3b).

Additionally, keep in mind that it is a hermeneutical error to read the modern-day situation back into the pages of Scripture, trying to force the proverbial square peg of the modern day into the round hole of the Old Testament Bible passage. Moreover, some of the statements that have been made about this passage even have a tendency to impose New Testament soteriology back into the Old Testament. In Bible interpretation, the appropriate way to apply a passage is first to find out what it meant in the Biblical author's/reader's own day and situation (historical interpretation), and then to understand the grammar and

---

17 In the book, *Measuring the Music: Another Look at the Contemporary Christian Music Debate*, John Makujina does an excellent job dealing with the exegesis of Bible passages in reference to music.

18 Carl Friedrich Keil and Franz Delitzsch, *Commentary on the Old Testament*, vol. 5 (Peabody, MA: Hendrickson, 1996), 300.

19 Tremper Longman III, *Psalms: An Introduction and Commentary*, ed. David G. Firth, vol. 15–16, Tyndale Old Testament Commentaries (Nottingham, England: Inter-Varsity Press, 2014), 187.

context of the passage. Only at that point can some equivalent parallels be drawn for application to our modern day.

"I was glad when they said unto me, Let us go into the house of the LORD." Ps. 122:1

Some years ago I recall being in a church that had this verse beautifully stenciled on the wall behind the platform. Although I appreciated the Scripture so prominently displayed in the auditorium, I think that great care needs to be taken concerning the believer's interpretation and application of this verse. Often Psalm 122:1 is used to teach how joyful we ought to be to attend church services. To those who use the verse this way, it is common to see "the house of the LORD" as a reference to the local church building. Many even refer to the church building this way, or just call it "God's house." The idea is that we as believers ought to rejoice and be glad as we come together in "church" (the building).

Although I appreciate the sentiment that believers should rejoice when they come together, this view of the passage brings up some serious hermeneutical questions. Is the "house of the LORD" a reference to the church building? Did the church even exist at this point in history? Can we still make a legitimate application of this verse to today's world?

A Grammatical Perspective

The Hebrew word for "house" in this text is *bayith*. Although the word has a plethora of meanings, the one definition that is significant for the passage under our consideration is the meaning of "temple." Wiersbe mentions its more specific meaning here: "The phrase 'house of God' was used for the tabernacle (1 Sam 1:7, 24; 2 Sam. 12:20), so it could certainly be used for the tent David pitched for the ark in Jerusalem (2 Sam. 6)."[20]

---

20 Warren W. Wiersbe, *Be Exultant*, 1st ed., "Be" Commentary Series (Colorado Springs, CO: Cook Communications Ministries, 2004), 149.

A Historical and Contextual Perspective

Verses 2ff indicate to us that this "house" of v. 1 is located in Jerusalem. The superscription reads, "A Song of degrees [ascents] of David." Merrill F. Unger, in introducing this section of the Psalms writes, "Psalms 129-134 bear the superscription, 'A song of degrees' correctly, 'Song of Ascents' or "Goings-Up.' Apparently, the correct view is that these fifteen psalms were sung by worshipers as they went up to Jerusalem to celebrate the three great festivals (Deut. 16:16)."[21] As the Deuteronomy passage mentions, these three great festivals were the Feast of Unleavened Bread, the Feast of Weeks, and the Feast of Tabernacles (Booths). Psalm 121 was sung as they approached the mountains around Jerusalem, and this psalm was sung within the gates of Jerusalem.

Thomas Constable writes of this psalm: "David spoke of his delight in going up to the temple to worship the LORD in this short psalm of Zion. He exhorted the Israelites to pray for the security of Jerusalem so that this blessing might continue."[22] Of vv. 1-2 Constable wrote, "David related how happy he felt when it was time to worship the LORD at the sanctuary in Jerusalem. It was a great privilege to stand within the gates of the city that Yahweh had chosen as the place where He would meet with His people."[23]

So, it is clear from the context that the "House of the LORD" is in Jerusalem, and it is where the presence of *Yahweh* dwells: the tabernacle/temple. The worship here is not from the church (which didn't begin until Acts 2), but Jewish worship under the Law (v. 4). In the psalm, for the sake of "the house of the LORD" the psalmist seeks the good of Jerusalem (v. 9). It is patently clear that Ps. 122:1 is not a reference to joy as one walks into the church building. Additionally, the local church is not "the house of the LORD," nor is the church building "the church"

---

21 Merrill F. Unger, "Psalms" in *Unger's Commentary on the Old Testament* (Chattanooga, TN: AMG Publishers, 2002), p. 943.

22 Thomas L. Constable, *Notes on Psalms* (No publisher mentioned on the PDF file, 2022), p. 445.

23 Ibid.

anyhow. The church is *the people* whom Jesus purchased with His own blood: "shepherd the church of God which He purchased with His own blood" (Acts 20:28b).

So, Can This Passage Be Applied to Us Today?

Of course, it can! We see from Psalm 122:1 that Old Testament worship was full of joy and thanksgiving, and focused on the Lord. Should not our worship have the same character today? Often the worship of today is either joyless, mechanical, and selfish; or sensual, emotional, and man-centered. What is often called worship is, in many cases, not "all about God," nor is it focused on Him. Much modern so-called worship focuses on man, and what pleases him and makes him feel good.

"Where there is no vision, the people perish." Proverbs 29:18a

I have heard more than one man preach Proverbs 29:18a this way: "What Christians need today is a vision of a lost world! Believers today are lacking *vision*, and that is why so many are perishing and going to a Christless hell, and 'Where *there* is **no** vision, the people **perish**.'" Although there is nothing intrinsically wrong with the statement just written, there is a problem with using Prov. 29:18a to support it! That is not the meaning that rises naturally from the text.

One of the most important principles of hermeneutics is that every text has only ONE meaning. The meaning of the Proverbs text under our consideration is clearly not "catching a vision of people perishing in a Christless eternity." There are at least a few hermeneutical errors that are committed to come up with this erroneous interpretation: word definition errors, which are also combined with contextual errors and historical errors.

The very first thing that should not ring true to your ear is that statement concerning a "Christless eternity." Keep in mind that this text was written under the dispensation of the Law. We cannot read New Testament doctrine back into the Old Testament. God has revealed Himself and His will to man *progressively*. At the time when Solomon penned these words, the Messiah had not yet come. They would have had no idea what a "Christless eternity" was at this point. That is the first thing that should make this interpretation suspect.

Going a little deeper, if we study the word translated "vision" (*chazon*), it will reveal that the word has very little to do with our common, modern English definition: "a vivid, imaginative conception or anticipation...."[24] The *NET Bible* notes are correct when they state that the Hebrew word *chazon* as used here, "refers to divine communication to prophets (as in 1 Sam 3:1) and not to individual goals or plans.[25]"

Equally important is the area of context. When the definition of the word is coupled with the context of the latter part of the verse ("but he that keepeth the <u>law</u>, happy *is* he"), it becomes apparent that this passage is not teaching that we need to "catch a vision of a lost world." The focus of the verse is not "anticipation" or "individual goals or plans," but *revelation*!

The "vision" in Proverbs 29:18 is a *prophet's vision*. As mentioned previously, 1 Samuel 3:1 speaks of this type of revelation: "And the child Samuel ministered unto the LORD before Eli. And the word of the LORD was precious in those days; *there was* no open **vision**." Derek Kidner wrote of Proverbs 29:18 that, "*Vision...*is to be taken in its exact sense of the revelation a prophet receives. *Law* in line 2 is its complement.[26]" So, the word "vision" as well as its complementary term, "law," indicates that the subject of this passage is *revelation from God*.

The word translated as "perish" is also often misunderstood. Some would equate it with the word translated "perish" in John 3:16. The

---

24 Definition #5 of "vision" from the Dictionary.com entry, https://www.dictionary.com/browse/vision, accessed July 20, 2021.

25 Biblical Studies Press, *The NET Bible First Edition; Bible. English. NET Bible.; The NET Bible* (Biblical Studies Press, 2005).

26 Derek Kidner, *Proverbs: An Introduction and Commentary*, vol. 17, Tyndale Old Testament Commentaries (Downers Grove, IL: InterVarsity Press, 1964), 168.

problem is that the term does not refer to eternal punishment. Instead, we need to understand the meaning of the Hebrew word *p¹ra±* as the *Theological Wordbook of the Old Testament* indicates: "'to let loose' in the sense of 'to let run wild' (Exo 32:25 [twice]), 'when Moses saw the people "so out of hand".'"[27] The author then gives a possible translation of this verse: "'Where there is no vision (revelation from God), the people are "undisciplined/get out of hand".'"[28] Delitzsch in his commentary translates the Hebrew word as "ungovernable," and suggests the meanings of "unrestrained" and "disorderly."[29] Kidner gives a similar idea when he translates the KJV word "perish," as "run wild."[30] He continues, "The verb means to let loose, e.g. to let one's hair down, whether literally (Lev. 13:45; Num. 5:18; Judg. 5:2) or figuratively (especially Exod. 32:25 [twice]: RV 'broken loose', etc.)."[31] Several of the modern versions translate *p¹ra±* as "cast off restraint."

The meaning and application of this passage become plain when the words and the contexts are clearly understood. The author was saying that "where there is no prophet's vision the people cast off restraint/run wild/get out of hand, but he that keeps the law is happy." Although the gift of prophecy is not in effect in our day, the modern application is obvious: when the Word of God is ignored or is not present among a people, those same people will live unrestrained lives. We can only find restraint and joyful living as the Word of God is studied and heeded.

"Behold, I have graven thee upon the palms of my hands." Is. 49:16a

Here is another verse that you will find written on certain Christian gifts. The implied meaning by those who take this verse out of context is that Christ died on the cross for our sins, and the nail marks on His hands were for us. In this sense, His children are engraved on the palms

---

27 Victor P. Hamilton under the word *p¹ra±, The Theological Wordbook of the Old Testament, Vol. 2* (Chicago: Moody Press, 1981), pp. 736-737.

28 Ibid., p. 737.

29 C.F. Keil and F. Delitzsch, *Commentary on the Old Testament Vol. VI* (Grand Rapids: William B. Eerdman's Publishing Company, 1986), pp. 251-252.

30 Kidner, p. 168.

31 Ibid.

of His hands. Because of this, He will not "forget" us or neglect us. We are special to Him.

It's significant to note that I have never seen this verse *in its entirety* etched on any plaque or gift. The second half of the verse is always ignored. If the entire verse were written, the meaning that some assign to the verse would no doubt be suspect: "Behold, I have graven thee upon the palms of *my* hands; thy walls *are* continually before me." This is clearly another contextual blunder. Once again, let's make some observations concerning the text:

- As far as historical interpretation is concerned, keep in mind that these words were written under the dispensation of the Law long before Christ died on the cross. Unless this is a prophecy (and there is no indication of that), it *cannot* be referring to Jesus Christ dying on the cross.

- Once again, the context also helps answer questions. Who is "thee" and "thy walls?" This must be a reference to the same person/people. Verse 14 makes it clear that He is speaking about Zion/Jerusalem; specifically, the Jewish people living there. Ryrie in his clear and concise manner puts the passage (vv. 14-26) together for us:

  Here the Lord encourages His people who will be in captivity. He has not forgotten them (vv. 14–18); He will restore them to their land (vv. 19–23) and punish their enemies (vv. 24–26). The return of such a large group described in verses 19–21 must look beyond the relatively small group that returned from Babylon to the second coming of Christ (Matt. 24:31).[32]

Before the days of setting cell phone alarms, I had the practice of writing things on my hand with an ink pen *so I wouldn't forget* an appointment that I had, or a task that had to be done. The hand was a conspicuous place, and as such was a constant reminder. Similarly, using

---

32 Charles Caldwell Ryrie, *Ryrie Study Bible: New American Standard Bible, 1995 Update*, Expanded ed. (Chicago: Moody Press, 1995), 1121.

a figure of speech, God had carved/inscribed God's people in Zion into the palms of His hands. He would not forget them: "Therefore whenever He, figuratively speaking, lifts up His hands He sees the nation's name which reminds Him of her.³³" The walls of the city were continually before Him. As God similarly promised them in the previous verse: "Can a woman forget her sucking child, that she should not have compassion on the son of her womb? yea, they may forget, yet will I not forget thee."

Isaiah 49:16a is clearly NOT speaking of the wounds on Christ's hands from the cross. It is promising those who dwell in Jerusalem that in the coming captivity they would not be forgotten. There was a bright future (for all Israel), not only following the captivity, but at the Second Coming of Christ as well.

As I have said, although this passage is not written _to_ today's reader, it still is _for_ us by way of careful application (cf. 1 Cor. 10:11). Clearly, we can find encouragement from this passage. We see here the promise-keeping character of our great God! We understand that because God did not forget His covenant people to whom He made definite promises, so He will not forget His children to whom He also made definite promises! Hebrews 13:5b declares, "I will never leave thee, nor forsake thee."

> *"For I know the thoughts that I think toward you, saith the LORD, thoughts of peace, and not of evil, to give you an expected end." Jer. 29:11*

I find with this twisted text that it is often quoted from the NIV: "'For I know the plans I have for you,' declares the LORD, 'plans to prosper you and not to harm you, plans to give you hope and a future.'"

This verse has become a part of "pop Christianity," and can be found in Christian gift outlets with the verse imprinted on key chains and display signs. Once again, some teach that the idea is that this was written to Christians to let them know that God thinks about us, and

---

33 John A. Martin, "Isaiah," in *The Bible Knowledge Commentary: An Exposition of the Scriptures*, ed. J. F. Walvoord and R. B. Zuck, vol. 1 (Wheaton, IL: Victor Books, 1985), 1104.

the thoughts that He thinks are those that will bring us peace and not evil in our life on earth, and plans for a glorious future with Him in eternity. So, is this what this verse means? As my dear friend, Dr. Clay Nuttall used to teach his students to ask: "What does the text say?" Remember we need to follow the process of observation, interpretation, and application.

There are things we have observed about the text through a cursory reading, but now we need to interpret the text. As we said earlier, one of the most important rules to follow in a normal hermeneutic is that of placing the passage in its proper context, both macro and micro. The verse under our consideration is a sentence within Jeremiah's letter to the Jews taken captive to Babylon. Ryrie does an excellent job placing vv. 1-23 in its proper context: "Sent to the 3,023 Jews who had been taken to Babylon in 597 B.C. (cf. 52:28) to exhort them to live as normal a life as possible (29:4–9), to await God's deliverance after 70 years (vv. 10–14), and to disregard false prophets such as *Ahab* and *Zedekiah* (v. 21).[34]" Generally, this information (contextual and historical information)[35] is all we need to know to answer a couple of questions and interpret this verse correctly.

- To whom was this verse written? Jews of the Babylonian captivity. This then explains who is addressed as "you" in v. 11.

- With this in mind, what exactly does the promise mean (as per the NIV): "plans to prosper you and not to harm you, plans to give you hope and a future?" Reading and understanding vv. 12-13 of this chapter helps us to understand what the prophet meant: "Then shall ye call upon me, and ye shall go and pray unto me, and I will hearken unto you. And ye shall seek me, and find *me*, when ye shall search for me with all your heart." F.B. Huey gives us the obvious meaning of this text:

---

34 Charles Caldwell Ryrie, *Ryrie Study Bible: New American Standard Bible, 1995 Update*, Expanded ed. (Chicago: Moody Press, 1995), 1201.

35 The grammar is not as significant here in this passage.

The Lord assured the people that what had happened was not a series of unplanned, accidental events. He said, "I know the plans" (lit. "I, I know"; emphatic in Heb.). His plan was not intended to hurt them but to give them "hope and a future" (perhaps a hendiadys, "a hopeful future"). He encouraged them to pray, for he would listen to them.[36]

The 70 years[37] of captivity in Babylon before God's people would return to Judah, was intended to discipline God's people and bring her to repentance, not to "harm" her. God intended in the future to make His chosen people prosperous, and to give them hope and a future. They would return to the land, and God would bless them. His plan for His people was not over (and still isn't!). In that great day when they return to the land, they would pray and God would listen. After the 70 years they would seek Him with all of their heart. A new section of the book of Jeremiah begins in chapter 30 where the prophet details the distant

---

36   F. B. Huey, *Jeremiah, Lamentations*, vol. 16, The New American Commentary (Nashville: Broadman & Holman Publishers, 1993), 254.

37   Seventy was not just a random number chosen by the Lord. In his explanation that the seventy-sevens of Daniel 9 are seventy-sevens of *years* (and not days or weeks), Renald Showers writes, ...seventy sevens of years would have been very meaningful to the Jews. God had divided their calendar into seven year periods with every seventh year being a sabbatic year (Lev. 25:3–9), and **their Babylonian captivity was to last seventy years because they had violated seventy sabbatic years over the course of 490 years (2 Chr. 36:21).** Daniel himself had been thinking in terms of years in the context of this prophecy (9:1–2). [Emphasis mine.] Renald E. Showers. *The Most High God: Commentary on the Book of Daniel* (Bellmawr, NJ: Friends of Israel Gospel Ministry, Inc., 1982), pp. 117-118.

Leon Wood concurs:

...the seventy-year period of captivity was based on the idea that seventy of these sabbatical years had not been kept (see 2 Chron. 36:21; cf. Lev. 26:33-35; Jer. 34:12-22). Knowing this, Daniel would have recognized that the seventy years of the captivity represented seventy sevens of years in which these violations had occurred; he would have understood Gabriel to be saying simply that another period, similar in length to that which had made the captivity necessary, was coming in the future experience of the people. [Emphasis mine.] Leon J. Wood. *Daniel* (Grand Rapids, MI: Zondervan Publishing House, 1975), pp. 116-117.

In essence *Yahweh* was taking back from Judah what she had refused to give Him over a 490-year time period: 70 sabbatical years. This in turn has bearing on Daniel's 70-years prophecy in Daniel 9 as the quotes demonstrate.

future restoration of all Israel at the end of the Tribulation Period and in the Millennial Kingdom.

- How should this passage be applied? After careful consideration I think the reader can see that this passage is obviously not a general promise to all believers today, and should never be taught or preached that way! The promise is specifically for God's people who were in captivity in Babylon. They were being assured that God was not done with them. He would bless them, and they would return to the land.

Clearly, this promise is not made to us. The church cannot claim the promises made to Israel. However, legitimate application *can* be made. Just as God was true to His promises with Israel, so we can trust Him to be true in fulfilling what He promised to us (1 Cor. 10:13; 1 Thess. 4:16-17; *et al.*). Yes, God has future plans and a hope for His church as well, but let's understand that this passage was not written *to* us, even though some application can be made *for* us. As faithful interpreters of God's Word we need to make sure that we always keep in mind the vast difference between the promises that God made to Israel, and the promises that God made to the church.

Chapter 7

TORTURED NEW TESTAMENT TEXTS

"The kingdom of God cometh not with observation: Neither shall they say, Lo here! or, lo there! for, behold, the kingdom of God is within you." **Luke 17:20b-21**

Some Amillennialists (and others of a Reformed persuasion) say that this passage refutes the teaching of a future, literal, earthly Kingdom for the Jews. They say that the premillennialists/dispensationalists are in error, and that the only Kingdom of God now is spiritual in nature; *not* literal. Moreover, they say that in our text Christ had to correct the misconception that the Jewish people had about the Kingdom when he stated that, "The kingdom of God cometh not with observation: Neither shall they say, Lo here! or, lo there!" This, they say demonstrates that although the Jewish people had the concept of an earthly, physical kingdom, Christ was correcting and instructing them that the kingdom was *spiritual* instead. Although the Jewish people were expecting their Messiah to burst on the scene and immediately grab the reins of government and destroy all of their enemies, Jesus had instead come to offer them a *spiritual* kingdom. In addition, some would say that the Church has replaced disobedient Israel. To clinch their argument, they continue to read the rest of the text which says that the kingdom of God is "within you," and is therefore not physical.

So, does this clinch the argument that the Kingdom is not earthly, temporal, and physical, but spiritual instead? No, not even close!

What the Text *Doesn't* Mean

I have taught my students through the years that although there may be times when we may have questions about what a passage means, most of the time we can at least determine what it *doesn't* mean. In those cases, the context clearly shows what the text is *not* teaching, although we may have some questions about what it *does* teach.

An obvious example of this principle may be found as we attempt to interpret 1 Cor. 15:29: "Else what shall they do which are baptized for the dead, if the dead rise not at all? why are they then baptized for the dead?" As David Lowery writes, "Up to 200 explanations have been given of this verse! Most of these interpretations are inane, prompted by a desire to conform this verse to an orthodox doctrine of baptism."[1] Although the exact meaning of this text may be unclear[2], what *is* clear from *many* Scriptures is that the text cannot be tacitly teaching the Mormon doctrine of baptism for the dead. The Bible clearly teaches that baptism is <u>not</u> something necessary for salvation. Furthermore, God's Word also plainly teaches that a person cannot vicariously experience salvation for someone else, particularly one who is dead. Our quest for the meaning of a text should not transport us to levels of absurdity that conflict with other clear passages in the Bible. We are to interpret the *unclear* in the light of the *clear*.

Similarly, at first glance, we may struggle with the exact meaning of Lk. 17:20b-21. However, it should be clear to us that Christ cannot be teaching that the Kingdom to which He refers in the Gospels is simply spiritual in nature; and therefore, cannot be literal, earthly, temporal, and Jewish. Using a normal/literal hermeneutic, we see many scriptures throughout the Bible that teach an earthly kingdom, including passages in the Gospels where our Lord in His earthly ministry never corrected the idea that the Jews had of this kind of kingdom. Moreover, the immediate context clearly repudiates the idea that Christ is teaching

---

1 David K. Lowery, "1 Corinthians," in *The Bible Knowledge Commentary: An Exposition of the Scriptures*, ed. J. F. Walvoord and R. B. Zuck, vol. 2 (Wheaton, IL: Victor Books, 1985), 544.

2 The author will not attempt to unravel that complex text here.

that there will only be a spiritual kingdom within the hearts of men. In fact, that is just the opposite of what He is relating to His listeners.

Without fully understanding what this text means, the spiritual kingdom idea is easily disproved by asking whom the Lord is addressing. Consider the text once again: "And when he was demanded of <u>the Pharisees</u>, when the kingdom of God should come, he answered them and said, The kingdom of God cometh not with observation:…for, behold, the kingdom of God is within you." Does it seem consistent of Jesus Christ to say to the ungodly, unbelieving, hypocritical Pharisees that the spiritual kingdom of God was within each one of them? These are the same Pharisees of which Christ said in Matt. 23:27: "Woe unto you, scribes and Pharisees, hypocrites! for ye are like unto whited sepulchres, which indeed appear beautiful outward, but are within full of dead *men's* bones, and of all uncleanness." Surely, if Christ were to speak of a spiritual kingdom of which all who know God are a part, He would <u>not</u> have pointed to the Pharisees and said, "The kingdom of God is within you." Clearly, the text is not teaching a spiritual kingdom in lieu of a literal kingdom. It should be clear what this text is NOT saying.

Some Background of the Text

So, we have unquestionably seen what the text is *not* teaching. What then is our Lord trying to communicate? Although this passage does not approach the complexity of 1 Cor. 15:29, in a similar way, seeing what it doesn't say is more obvious than what it does say. Before we see what our Lord is saying, there is some background to the text that we need to understand. As we clarify the meaning of this passage, keep in mind that the forerunner of Jesus Christ, John the Baptist had declared that the nation needed to prepare for the Messiah: "Repent ye: for the kingdom of heaven is at hand." (Matt. 3:2b). The literal, earthly Kingdom as promised in the Old Testament was at that time being offered to the

Jews. Jesus Himself repeated that same message (Matt. 4:17), as did the Twelve (Matt. 10:6-7) and the 70 (Lk. 10:9, 11).[3]

Matthew 12 is pivotal to this offer of the kingdom to the Jewish people. J. Dwight Pentecost writes, "This incident, then marked the great turning point in the life of Christ. From this point on to the cross the nation is viewed in the Gospels as having rejected Christ as Messiah. The unofficial rejection by the leaders would become official when finalized at the cross."[4] The leadership at this point completely rejected their Messiah, King, and Kingdom by attributing the miracles of Christ, as wrought by the Holy Spirit (v. 28) to Satan (Beelzebub, v. 24). This was the final rejection of Christ and the offer of the Kingdom. They had rejected the testimony and message of who Jesus was, and had also rejected the testimony of the Father (Matt. 3:17; John 14:10). Now, they were rejecting the testimony of the Holy Spirit by attributing the miracle of casting out demons to Satan himself. This ultimate rejection could not be forgiven (Matt 12:31-32) because no other testimony was possible![5]

As a result of this ultimate rejection, the literal, earthly, temporal kingdom was "postponed." It is clear that the kingdom was not postponed in the plan of a sovereign God, as if He were taken by surprise. It was, however, postponed from *man's point of view*. The kingdom was offered, rejected, and postponed to a yet future day when Christ will return to earth a second time to set up His promised kingdom and fulfill the covenants that He made with His people, Israel. Pentecost does an excellent job summarizing the ideas in Matthew 12:

---

3 I have not attempted to give a defense of my position on the "postponement" of the Kingdom, since it is beyond the scope of this book. For a thorough argument for the "postponement" of the Kingdom, please see J. Dwight Pentecost, "The Kingdom Offered—and Rejected" (chapter 18), in *Thy Kingdom Come: Tracing God's Kingdom Program and Covenant Promises Throughout History* (Grand Rapids: Kregel Publications, 1995); and Charles C. Ryrie, "Dispensational Eschatology" (chapter 8), in *Dispensationalism: Revised and Expanded* (Chicago: Moody Press, 1995).

4 J. Dwight Pentecost. *The Words and Works of Jesus Christ: A Study of the Life of Christ* (Grand Rapids, Zondervan Publishing House, 1981), 208.

5 I don't believe that this unique sin can be committed today.

Jerusalem would come under judgment (24:37-39) and would fall to the Gentiles (Luke 21:24). From this point on Christ no longer publicly announced that the kingdom was at hand; instead, He indicated that the kingdom had been postponed. He was not anticipating a throne, but instead foresaw a cross. What He had originally come to fulfill in God's covenant program for Israel had been postponed until another coming.[6]

Chronologically, the incident with the Pharisees in Luke 17 takes place some time after the nation's ultimate rejection of Christ. The Jewish people however had not come to the realization of a postponed kingdom.

What the Text <u>Is</u> Teaching

Under what circumstances did the events of this passage occur? Keep in mind that Christ is answering a question from the Pharisees. They had heard it preached from the very mouth of Jesus that the Kingdom of God was at hand. Now, they wanted to know more specifically *when* the Kingdom was going to come. Additionally, notice that this is a *Jewish* question addressed to the *Jewish* people. In response to the Pharisees, Christ communicated two basic ideas. The NIV (1984) has an interesting translation that does a good job of contrasting these two ideas, and highlights the difference between verse 20 and verse 21:

> Once, having been asked by the Pharisees when the kingdom of God would come, Jesus replied, "The kingdom of God does not come with **your** careful observation [the Pharisees], [21] nor will **people** [the Jewish people in general] say, 'Here it is,' or 'There it is,' because the kingdom of God is within you."[7]

In the first part of our Lord's reply, He says, "The kingdom of God does not come with your careful observation nor will people say, 'Here it

---

6 J. Dwight Pentecost, *Thy Kingdom Come: Tracing God's Kingdom Program and Covenant Promises Throughout History* (Grand Rapids: Kregel Publications, 1995), p. 219.

7 Robert Deffinbaugh points out the contrast here between the Pharisees and the Jewish people in general in his digital commentary on Luke (Robert Deffinbaugh. *Luke: The Gospel of the Gentiles* (Richardson, TX: Biblical Studies Press, 1996), p. 491.

is,' or 'There it is.'" The fact is that neither the Pharisees nor the rest of the Jewish people would be able to detect signs or see the Messiah coming into His kingdom at this point. The kingdom had been postponed.

The translation of the last part of the statement in the 1984 NIV, "because the kingdom of God is <u>within you</u>," is probably not correct. The updated (2011) NIV (along with other modern translations) is better here[8]: "Because the kingdom of God is <u>in your midst</u>." Keep in mind that isolating language from the context is bad hermeneutical practice. Language and context must work together in harmony. Although it is permissible for the Greek word in isolation to be translated "the kingdom of God is <u>within</u> you," it does not fit the context. The alternate meaning of the adverb is "among" or "in the midst of," and fits the context better here. The King was in their midst. This made the kingdom possible, but it would not happen at that time because they had rejected the Lord Jesus Christ.

J. Dwight Pentecost does an excellent job interpreting and explaining the meaning of our text:

> Christ was not signifying that the kingdom He had come to institute was only a spiritual rule in the hearts of people. Rather, He meant that because of Israel's rejection, the kingdom would not come literally and physically and visibly at that time. Christ did state, "the kingdom of God is within you" (Luke 17:21). However, the Greek word translated "within you" literally means "in your midst," or "among" (NIV margin). Christ was affirming that because the King was present, the kingdom was possible. The Pharisees' question implied that kingdom was impossible because the leaders did not accept Christ. But Christ affirmed that the kingdom was possible and was being offered because the King was present.
>
> Jesus revealed to His disciples that the kingdom anticipated by the prophets and offered by the Lord Himself would be postponed. Hence He said they would not "see one of the days

---

8 Although I generally dislike the 2011 revision of the NIV.

of the Son of Man" (v. 22). Many false Messiah's would appear and claim to fulfill the kingdom He promised, but the disciples were not to be deceived (v. 23). They were to remember that the kingdom had been postponed until a future time. When the time arrived for the institution of the future Davidic millennial kingdom, people will know it. Jesus said, "The Son of Man in His day will be like lightening" (v. 24)....[9]

So we see from an understanding of the background, grammar, and context of this passage that Christ is neither teaching that the literal, earthly kingdom has been abolished, nor that the kingdom that Christ offered was only a spiritual one. This passage simply tells the Pharisees that although the presence of the King in their midst made the earthly kingdom possible, the fact that they had rejected Him meant that there would be no earthly kingdom (which would be detectable by signs) at this time. It would be postponed until a later time.

"Jesus answered and said unto him, Verily, verily, I say unto thee, Except a man be born again, he cannot see the kingdom of God." John 3:3

I have included the analysis of this passage in this section of the book, although it is quite different from the other twisted and tortured texts. Some differences of opinion exist concerning this passage, not just because of simple, careless hermeneutical errors. Good, solid men who hold staunchly to a normal hermeneutic have disagreements concerning this passage.

Having said that, I would like to explain how I resolved my struggle with this text, and how I came to the conclusions that I did.

Common Teaching Concerning John 3

"In John 3 Jesus calls on Nicodemus to be 'born again,' a term referring to regeneration. The events of this passage occur before Acts 2, and even before the death of Jesus Christ. Not only does this passage

---

9 J. Dwight Pentecost. *The Words and Works of Jesus Christ: A Study of the Life of Christ* (Grand Rapids, Zondervan Publishing House, 1981), p. 349.

indicate that regeneration occurred before the coming of the Holy Spirit and the formation of the Church, it also indicates that regeneration was normative in the Old Testament. After all, how could we talk about the salvation of Old Testament saints without regeneration? This passage is proof positive that Old Testament saints experienced regeneration."

There is one other issue that goes hand-in-hand with the teaching that John three indicates that Old Testament saints were regenerated. It is found in verse three. There, Christ tells Nicodemus that unless one is regenerated, he cannot see the kingdom of God. To be consistent with the teaching on regeneration that I just presented, they say that the "kingdom of God" must be a reference to a spiritual (not a literal, temporal, earthly) kingdom.

Arnold Fruchtenbaum, although a solid premillennial dispensationalist, holds to the John 3 position to which I am referring[10]:

> The Spiritual Kingdom is composed of all who have experienced the new birth in all times by the Holy Spirit. From Adam until our day and as long as men continue to be born on this earth there will be the existence of the Spiritual Kingdom. Every individual since Adam onward who has been born again by faith through the regenerating work of the Holy Spirit is a member of this kingdom. This is the Kingdom of God that Jesus spoke of to Nicodemus when He said that unless one is born again he cannot see, he cannot enter into the Kingdom of God. This is God's rule in the heart of the believer.[11]

My Struggle with the Passage

As will be made obvious, I do not agree with the previous view of John 3. Until about 30 years ago the spiritual kingdom view of John 3 was all that I knew, even though it didn't really make sense. In v. 10 our Lord asks Nicodemus "Art thou a master [teacher] of Israel, and knowest not these things?" One thing that didn't make sense was that

---

10 There are many other solid dispensationalists who hold to this same position.
11 Arnold G. Fruchtenbaum, *Israelology: The Missing Link in Systematic Theology*, Rev. ed. (Tustin, CA: Ariel Ministries, 1994), 610.

Nicodemus was rebuked by the Lord because he should have known from the Old Testament scriptures that a person needed regeneration to enter the spiritual kingdom. That made no sense to me, considering that there is no clear passage in the Old Testament that speaks of regeneration opening up the way into the spiritual kingdom. I did, however, find Old Testament passages that dealt with regeneration *in the light of the New Covenant*[12] and entrance into the *earthly* kingdom. That last discovery began to open up the meaning of this passage to me.

I began looking for studies on John 3 that might shed some light on this difficult passage and clear up some of my confusion. I came upon a simple, yet thought-provoking book by Herman A. Hoyt: *Expository Messages on the New Birth* (sadly out of print, I believe). As I read Hoyt's messages and studied John 3, I came to the realization that the passages that reveal regeneration in the Old Testament are indeed related to the New Covenant, and that the truths Christ was presenting in relationship to this are what Nicodemus should have known. This connection with the New Covenant even opened up the meaning of a verse that I found very confusing: verse 5, which mentions being born of *the water* and of *the Spirit*.

In the rest of this section, I want to explain what I believe John 3 is teaching. Perhaps the nuggets of truth in this section will help you to come to the same conclusions that I did.

Introductory Remarks on John 3:1-21

Were Old Testament Saints Regenerated?

Keep in mind that the careful student of Scripture should never take New Testament doctrine and read it back into the Old Testament. We need to accept what rises naturally from the text, even if it doesn't completely fit our present theological scheme. Without adequate Old Testament evidence of it, you often hear people argue, "The Old Testament saints must have been regenerated. It's the only way they

---

12 The purpose of this work is not to discuss the New Covenant. If you would like more information on the New Covenant, I would suggest reading appropriate sections from *Thy Kingdom Come* by J. Dwight Pentecost (especially, chapter 15).

could have been saved!" That is definitely true today, but it may not have been true in the past. We cannot read back what is normative in this dispensation into previous dispensations just because we don't understand the past operation of God.

I agree with Herman Hoyt who rejects regeneration of Old Testament saints. He writes,

> Nor during the long Old Testament period did any man ever experience the new birth. This does not mean that there was not a ministry of the Holy Spirit to men during the Old Testament dispensation. It does mean that this ministry is not the same experience men have had since the coming of Christ. As far as can be determined the ministry of the Spirit had to do with function and office of the person involved....But in all the Old Testament revelation it seems quite evident that the experience of the Old Testament saints is not to be equated with the new birth which initiates the permanent indwelling of the Spirit. This alone explains the fact that the Holy Spirit departed from Saul (1 Sam 16:14), and the cry of David, "Cast me not away from thy presence; and take not thy holy Spirit from me" (Ps 51:11).[13]

Hoyt also brings up the fact that regeneration is dependent on the cross, therefore it could not have happened before that time: "Clearly enough, this work of God depended upon Christ's dealing with sin at Calvary. As long as sin separated between God and men, He could not in holiness enter into immediate and vital relationship with sinful creatures (Isa 59:1–2)."[14]

I believe the evidence shows that salvation in the Old Testament did not include what we know today as regeneration. This is particularly evident because, as Hoyt points out, there is a connection between regeneration and the permanent indwelling of the Holy Spirit.

---

13 Herman A. Hoyt, "Introduction to the Study of the New Birth," *Grace Journal* 1, no. 1 (1960): 22.
14 Ibid, p. 23.

Furthermore, permanent indwelling did not take place until Acts 2 (Jn. 14:17 -- "...for he dwelleth with you, and shall be in you").

The Purpose of John's Gospel

John 20:31 gives us the main purpose of why this gospel was written: "But these are written, that ye might believe that Jesus is the Christ, the Son of God; and that believing ye might have life through his name." So, the fourth gospel presents Jesus as both the Messiah as well as God incarnate. This was presented so readers might place their faith in Christ.

Edwin Blum goes on to explain the content of the gospel of John, which is consistent with the purpose that John mentions in 20:31:

> The major body of the Gospel is contained in a "Book of Signs" (2:1–12:50) which embraces seven miracles or "signs" which proclaim Jesus as the Messiah, the Son of God. This "Book of Signs" also contains great discourses of Jesus which explain and proclaim the significance of the signs. For example, following the feeding of the 5,000 (6:1–15), Jesus revealed Himself as the Bread of Life which the heavenly Father gives for the life of the world (6:25–35). Another notable and exclusive feature of the Fourth Gospel is the series of "I am" statements that were made by Jesus (cf. 6:35; 8:12; 10:7, 9, 11, 14; 11:25; 14:6; 15:1, 5).[15]

As we analyze the passage in front of us, we need to keep in mind that John 3 contributes to the main purpose of the book.

Who Was Nicodemus, and What Was the Purpose of His Visit?

All we know about this man is given in the gospel of John. 3:1 says that *he was a Pharisee*, and as such was a member of a Jewish sect that was the most orthodox of the day. The text also says that he was "a ruler of the Jews," denoting that he was a member of the very powerful

---

15 Edwin A. Blum, "John," in *The Bible Knowledge Commentary: An Exposition of the Scriptures*, ed. J. F. Walvoord and R. B. Zuck, vol. 2 (Wheaton, IL: Victor Books, 1985), 268.

Sanhedrin. Additionally, in v. 10, Jesus calls him <u>the</u> (the article is present in Greek) "master" or "teacher" in Israel. This may have some significance as Kent points out: "The text of 3:10 reads: 'Are you *the* teacher of Israel?' Therefore he may have been unique in some respect, perhaps as the most popular lecturer of his day."[16, 17]

We also see that Nicodemus came to Jesus by night. Why? Although the text does not specify, it has been speculated that as a member of the Sanhedrin he may have been afraid of the negative responses of others. That seems unlikely considering the boldness of Nicodemus in standing up for Jesus in 7:50-51, as well as his boldness in assisting in Jesus' burial in 19:38-40. It is perhaps more likely that he wanted to speak with Jesus at a time when there would be no distractions from the crowds that often surrounded Him. Additionally, Carson reminds us that "rabbis studied and debated long into the night."[18] As far as why John even mentions that it was night here, Carson makes a good point when he writes,

> The best clue lies in John's use of 'night' elsewhere: in each instance (3:2; 9:4; 11:10; 13:30) the word is either used metaphorically for moral and spiritual darkness, or, if it refers to the night-time hours, it bears the same moral and spiritual symbolism. Doubtless Nicodemus approached Jesus at night, but his own 'night' was blacker than he knew (*cf.* Hengstenberg, 1.157–158; Lightfoot, p. 116).[19]

It's also important to understand the purpose of Nicodemus' visit. Although the text does not clearly reveal why he came, or what he had

---

16 Homer A. Kent Jr., *Light in the Darkness: Studies in the Gospel of John*, Second Edition., The Kent Collection (Winona Lake, IN: BMH Books, 2010), 52.

17 In the footnote Kent adds, "Although this may be the case, in the footnote, Kent adds, "It is possible, of course, that "the teacher" is an instance of the generic use of the article, with the sense, "You occupy the position of the teacher, not the pupil; hence you should know these things."

18 D. A. Carson, *The Gospel according to John*, The Pillar New Testament Commentary (Leicester, England; Grand Rapids, MI: Inter-Varsity Press; W.B. Eerdmans, 1991), 186.

19 Ibid.

on his mind, there are some indicators from the context and culture of the day which help us to piece together the reason why he may have visited Jesus that night. J. Dwight Pentecost does a good job fitting together the pieces of the puzzle:

> Jesus, of whom it was said, "He did not need man's testimony about man, for he knew what was in man" (John 2:25), perceived the question that was uppermost in Nicodemus' mind. Nicodemus knew that Jesus was offering a prophesied kingdom. Nicodemus as a scholar of the law knew that the Old Testament required righteousness as a prerequisite for entrance into Messiah's kingdom (Ps. 24:3–4). Nicodemus was a Pharisee concerned about matters of the law, and he constantly considered how a man could be righteous before the law. Hence the following questions must have been on his mind at the offset: "How righteous does a man have to be to enter the kingdom?" "How can one enter Messiah's kingdom?" "How can one satisfy the demands of the law?" Christ's answer was pointed: "Unless a man is born again, he cannot see the kingdom of God" (John 3:3).[20]

Apparently, the idea of the *earthly messianic kingdom* is at the forefront of what Nicodemus is thinking. The idea of a spiritual or heavenly kingdom would NOT have been what Nicodemus was mulling over in his mind. Christ, in His interaction with Nicodemus, discusses this earthly kingdom and the *spiritual state* of the one who is qualified to enter it: "Except a man be born again, he cannot see the kingdom of God" (3:3). Additionally, Nicodemus seems to be representing others in the Sanhedrin who seem to have similar questions (v. 2 – "we know").

The Importance of the Layout of the Passage

One of the keys to interpreting this passage is to understand where the incident concerning Nicodemus and Jesus ends, and where the

---

20 J. Dwight Pentecost, *The Words & Works of Jesus Christ: A Study of the Life of Christ*, ed. John Danilson (Grand Rapids, MI: Zondervan, 1981), 124.

application of the events and commentary by John begins. D.A. Carson is spot on in his evaluation of the structure of the text:

> In vv. 1–21, the words of Jesus probably trail off at the end of v. 15, to be followed by the meditation of the Evangelist in vv. 16–21.... Similarly in vv. 22–36: the words of John the Baptist probably terminate with v. 30, while vv. 31–36 preserve a balancing meditation by the Evangelist on what has just been reported.[21]

A bit later in his commentary Carson continues the discussion:

> In two passages in this Gospel, both in this chapter (3:15–21 and 3:31–36), the words of a speaker (Jesus and John the Baptist respectively) are succeeded by the explanatory reflections of the Evangelist. Because the ancient texts did not use quotation marks or other orthographical equivalents, the exact point of transition is disputed....But vv. 16–21 read more plausibly as the Evangelist's meditation. For instance, the expression 'one and only' (*monogenēs*) is a word used by the Evangelist (1:14, 18; *cf.* 1 Jn. 4:9), and is not elsewhere placed on the lips of Jesus or of anyone else in this Gospel. Nor does Jesus normally refer to God as *ho theos* ('God')."[22]

As we begin to look at our text in more detail, we need to keep in mind that the account of Nicodemus' night meeting with Jesus probably concludes with v. 15, and John's extended comments and application of the story follows in vv. 16-21. His commentary on the meeting between Nicodemus and Jesus is completely in line with the purpose of the book as we mentioned earlier: "But these are written, that ye might believe that Jesus is the Christ, the Son of God; and that believing ye might have life through his name" (20:31).

---

21 Carson, p. 185.
22 Ibid, p. 203.

Some Key Expository Comments on the Text

The Account of Nicodemus' Night Meeting with Jesus (vv. 1-15)

My goal is not to give the reader a full commentary on these verses, but just to deal with relevant verses that highlight our point.

In verse two we see Nicodemus addressing Christ as "Rabbi." The term is "used in the NT as a respectful term of address for a scribe or one recognized as an outstanding teacher of the law."[23]

His understanding of the identity of this Man is revealed in the very next statement: "we know that thou art a teacher come from God: for no man can do these miracles that thou doest, except God be with him." Although Nicodemus is not confessing him to be the Messiah, at least he sees Him as One who has come from God. Furthermore, he has been convinced by the miracles that Jesus has performed that God is with Him. As we mentioned earlier, it is remarkable indeed that Nicodemus does not seem to be the only one convinced of these things, for he uses the pronoun "we." It seems there were others in the Sanhedrin who were convinced that this Man was a teacher come from God. J. Dwight Pentecost writes,

> Nicodemus was putting himself in the position of a learner seeking to inquire about the great truths that Christ had been teaching. Nicodemus had been motivated to come and present his inquiry because of the miraculous signs that Jesus had been performing. As the Sanhedrin debated these signs, at least a portion of the Sanhedrin had been forced to the conclusion that these signs were supernatural, not natural.[24]

In verse 3, without a word of explanation from Nicodemus, the omniscient Son of God, knowing this man intimately, cuts right to the

---

23 Timothy Friberg, Barbara Friberg, and Neva F. Miller, *Analytical Lexicon to the Greek New Testament*, Baker's Greek New Testament Library (Grand Rapids: Baker, 2000), Entry 23900, ῥαββί, ὁ; BibleWorks, v. 10.
24 Pentecost, p. 123.

heart of the matter.[25] Our Lord says, "Verily, verily, I say unto thee, Except a man be born again, he cannot see the kingdom of God." As we said earlier, the idea of the *earthly messianic kingdom* is what concerns Nicodemus. Neither Nicodemus nor Jesus is referring to a spiritual kingdom. As a good Jew and member of the Sanhedrin, Nicodemus is wondering about entrance into the literal, earthly, temporal kingdom. Christ in His reply is not changing kingdoms. He continues to talk with Nicodemus about exactly the same kingdom.

The misunderstanding that occurs between the two men is not over kingdoms (spiritual vs. earthly), but over the meaning of the term "born again" (*gennēthē anōthen*). The Greek term, *gennēthē anōthen* could either be translated "born again," or "born from above;" and although both meanings are probably meant in John 3, it is clear that Nicodemus is thinking of the former meaning. What he *doesn't* understand is that when Jesus tells him that he must be "born again," he is not referring to *physical* birth, but *spiritual* birth. Jesus is speaking of a doctrine we know in English as *regeneration*. The actual word, "regeneration" is used in Titus 3:5, and is a translation of the Greek word, *palingenesia,* which means "born again."

So, Christ is telling this night visitor that if anyone would enter the literal, earthly kingdom he would have to be regenerated. Just what is the significance of Christ's connecting regeneration with the Messianic kingdom? Christ tells Nicodemus that as "the teacher of Israel" he should have been familiar with what He was declaring to him. Is the Lord saying that Nicodemus should have been familiar with entering the spiritual kingdom through regeneration? Hardly. What he should have been familiar with as an Old Testament scholar was *the need for regeneration to enter the literal, Messianic kingdom.* The Old Testament

---

25 Once again, this display of omniscience is consistent with John's theme of presenting Jesus as the Son of God.

passages concerning the New Covenant[26](as opposed to the Old Covenant/Mosaic covenant: Jer. 31:31-32) clearly taught this. Notice:

> [24] For I will take you from among the heathen, and gather you out of all countries, and will bring you into your own land. [25] Then will I sprinkle clean water upon you, and ye shall be clean: from all your filthiness, and from all your idols, will I cleanse you. [26] A new heart also will I give you, and a new spirit will I put within you: and I will take away the stony heart out of your flesh, and I will give you an heart of flesh. [27] And I will put my spirit within you, and cause you to walk in my statutes, and ye shall keep my judgments, and do *them*. [28] And ye shall dwell in the land that I gave to your fathers; and ye shall be my people, and I will be your God. (Ezek. 36:24-28)

Notice that Israel:

1. Will be regathered in the land (v. 24);

2. Will be cleansed (v. 25);

3. **Will experience regeneration (v. 26);**

4. Will experience the indwelling Holy Spirit--**which goes with regeneration** (v. 27);

5. Will dwell in the land (v. 28).

Jer. 31:33 and 32:40 also mention this radical heart change. This heart change is taught in the Old Testament in the new covenant passages, and is called regeneration and the new birth in the New Testament. This is what is necessary to enter the Messiah's Kingdom. This is what should have been familiar to an Old Testament scholar like Nicodemus. It wasn't the externals, or self-righteousness, or birthright of the Pharisees that would qualify them for entrance into Messiah's

---

26 Keep in mind that God's key covenant with His people, Israel is the Abrahamic Covenant. Three aspects of this covenant are expanded by three other covenants. The *land* promises of the Abrahamic Covenant are explained and expanded in the Palestinian (Land) Covenant. The *seed* promises of the Abrahamic Covenant are explained and expanded in the Davidic Covenant. Last, the *blessing* promises are explained and expanded in the New Covenant. All four covenants are unconditional.

kingdom; it was a regenerated heart. Keep in mind too that the new covenant will not be fulfilled until the second coming.[27] This is therefore not a proof of regeneration taking place in the Old Testament.

As we enter v. 4, we see that Nicodemus had no idea what Jesus was talking about. This all sounded so absurd to him: "How can a man be born when he is old? can he enter the second time into his mother's womb, and be born?"

In v. 5 Christ clarifies what He means by *gennēthē anōthen* ("born again"). There has been much discussion through the years concerning the meaning of "born of water," but it becomes quite simple when we see this text's relationship to Ezek. 36:24-28 and the new covenant. Homer Kent explains the connection:

> ...To be a part of God's kingdom, one must be born "of water and of the Spirit." The similarity of this passage to Ezekiel 36:25–26 is striking. There God foretold what would someday happen to Israel when the nation would finally forsake sin and turn to God. "Then I will sprinkle clean water on you, and you will be clean ... from all your filthiness ... I will ... put a new spirit within you." The water symbolized the cleansing aspect of this experience, and the new spirit referred to the imparting of new life by the entrance of the Holy Spirit into the life.[28]

Hoyt does a good job laying out the Greek to support his understanding of "water and Spirit." He then concludes that "water and Spirit" relate to the Ezek. 36 passage that we just saw. As an expert in the scriptures Nicodemus should have known these things since they were revealed 600 years before by the prophet Ezekiel (v. 10). Hoyt mentions the Ezekiel passage in relationship to John 3: "In this prophecy of long ago, the words water and spirit appear. It is clear that the water is for cleansing, and the spirit is for quickening. The cleansing will proceed

---

27 Keep in mind that at this time the offer of the Messianic kingdom was still on the table ("repent for the kingdom of heaven is at hand"). It would not be until later that the kingdom would be "postponed" (from man's viewpoint, not God's—Matt. 12).

28 Homer A. Kent Jr., *Light in the Darkness: Studies in the Gospel of John*, Second Edition., The Kent Collection (Winona Lake, IN: BMH Books, 2010), 55.

from the statutes and judgments they will obey, and the new heart will be experienced from the presence of the Spirit of God within."[29]

So, no one will be able to enter the Messianic kingdom unless he is "born again/regenerated," which may be explained as being "born of water and *of* the Spirit." This is what the new covenant indicates as laid out in Ezekiel 36. Water refers to cleansing from sin (Ezek. 36:25), and "Spirit" refers to the indwelling Holy Spirit who makes alive (Ezek. 36:27). In our John 3 passage "water" and "Spirit" refer to the same.

Notice that Ezek. 36:28 says that those who experience this transformation, "will live in the land that I gave to your forefathers; so you will be My people, and I will be your God." They will enter the Kingdom because they are born again — they are regenerated! Further, v. 35 says, "They will say, 'This desolate land has become like the garden of Eden; and the waste, desolate and ruined cities are fortified *and* inhabited.'" It is no wonder this time is called "the regeneration" in Matt. 19:28. Those who enter the Kingdom will be given new life, and so will all creation!

Nicodemus needed to understand that the entrance into Christ's literal, earthly kingdom is only available to those who are regenerated. This is the answer to the question that was within the heart of this man who was searching for answers.

In v. 7 it is interesting to note that "ye" here is not singular, as would be expected if Jesus were talking only to Nicodemus. The pronoun is plural. I believe He is referring to Israel. Nicodemus was not to marvel that only those Jews (including himself) who were regenerated would enter the Kingdom as per what the New Covenant stated. The same plural pronouns are used in vv. 11-12.

---

29 Herman A. Hoyt, "The Explanation of the New Birth," *Grace Journal* 8, no. 2 (1967): 21.

The Application and Commentary
of the Apostle John (vv. 16-21)

As I said earlier, I believe the discussion between Christ and Nicodemus ends in v. 15, and vv. 16-21 contains the commentary of the Apostle John. This section also fulfills the purpose of the writing of this book. By applying the story of Nicodemus to his readers he wants them to "believe that Jesus is the Christ, the Son of God," and so by believing they might "have life through His name."

The New Covenant and regeneration are both based on the shed blood of the Lord Jesus Christ on the cross (1 Cor. 11:25; Titus 3:5-6). Although the New Covenant is for Israel alone, and concerns the future kingdom, we today *benefit* from that covenant because of the cross. Moreover, regeneration is not just something that prepares Israel for entrance into the kingdom. New life in Christ is something that a person in this dispensation can experience by believing in Him (1 Pet. 1:23). John begins his commentary and application section by giving a clear gospel message: "For God so loved the world, that he gave his only begotten Son, that whosoever believeth in him should not perish, but have everlasting life" (John 3:16).

Conclusions

I do not believe John 3 teaches that Old Testament saints were regenerated. In that section of Scripture Jesus is dealing with a member of the Sanhedrin who had some questions about qualifications to enter Messiah's earthly kingdom (not a spiritual kingdom). According to the Lord, anyone who enters Messiah's kingdom must be regenerated. This is consistent with what a scholar such as Nicodemus should have known from the New Covenant passages in the Old Testament (Ezek. 36). Finally, in vv. 16-21 John applies and elaborates on the Nicodemus incident to explain the need for regeneration today. Anyone who believes on Christ today can have regeneration and eternal life.

"Abstain from all appearance of evil." 1 Thess. 5:22

You are out to eat with your family. The order is taking a bit longer than the patience of your children. Two of your kids are getting restless and bored, and so, rip up the paper placemat in front of them. They begin to roll up sections of the place mat like cigarettes, and pretend to smoke them. Immediately, you stop them and rebuke them: "The Bible tells us in 1 Thessalonians 5:22 to 'Abstain from all appearance of evil.' What you are doing has the *appearance* of something that is evil, so you need to stop." Although you have rightfully rebuked them, you have wrongfully used the Scriptures.

I don't think that anyone who takes the Word of God or his testimony seriously would disagree that it is wrong for your kids to pretend like they are smoking. The problem with this scenario has to do with the *proof text* that you used to tell them to stop. Is 1 Thess. 5:22 instructing us not to do anything that might look evil to someone else? If this is true, then Mark 2:16 indicates that the Lord Jesus Christ contradicted that principle: "And when the scribes and Pharisees saw him eat with publicans and sinners, they said unto his disciples, How is it that he eateth and drinketh with publicans and sinners?" Was not Christ doing something that *looked* evil to someone else?

Unfortunately, there is a common misunderstanding of the English text of 1 Thessalonians 5:22. Hiebert mentions the struggle with the English text of the KJV, and he is spot on:

> But the rendering "all appearance of evil" (KJV) must not be interpreted to mean that they are to avoid that which *looks* wicked to those who see it, although in itself it may not be so. The term does not denote semblance as opposed to reality. Such a dictum might enable them to shun some unpleasant duty. "It is a poor heart that is much afraid of *seeming* evil in a good cause."[30] While believers should abstain from actions that will knowingly offend others, it is not always possible to

---

30 R. Mackintosh, *Thessalonians and Corinthians*, Westminster New Testament, p. 65.

abstain from everything that may appear evil to a narrow and foolish judgment.[31]

There are times when every believer will contradict the principle of "not doing anything that looks evil to someone else," and yet we will still be doing what is right and holy. Then, how are we to understand 1 Thess. 5:22? The context of the passage, as well as the meaning of the word translated "appearance" in the KJV is important if we are to comprehend the intent of the text.

The Context

Philip Comfort mentions in his commentary on 1 Thessalonians that chapter 5:12-22, "presents a series of staccato exhortations, a typical feature of New Testament epistles. This is a hefty list of exhortations, 17 in all, which can be arranged in the following groups:...."[32] Comfort then lists the following four divisions:

1. Attitudes and actions toward church leaders (5:12–13)....[33]
2. Attitudes and actions toward others (5:14–15)....[34]
3. Self-attitudes and actions (5:16–18)....[35]
4. Attitudes and actions about prophecy (5:19–22)[36]

The last section is most important to our understanding of v. 22. Hiebert entitles those verses in his outline, *"Principles for corporate spiritual life."*[37] So, 1 Thess. 5:19-22 deals with the spiritual life of the Thessalonian church, and their attitudes and actions toward the gift of prophecy. Keep in mind that prior to the completion of the New Testament canon, the gift of prophecy was extremely important to the first-century church. In fact, Ephesians 2:20 pairs the New Testament

---

31 D. Edmond Hiebert, *1 & 2 Thessalonians*, Revised Edition. (Winona Lake, IN: BMH Books, 1996), 266.

32 Harold W. Hoehner, Philip W. Comfort, and Peter H. Davids, *Cornerstone Biblical Commentary: Ephesians, Philippians, Colossians, 1&2 Thessalonians, Philemon.*, vol. 16 (Carol Stream, IL: Tyndale House Publishers, 2008), 374.

33 Ibid.

34 Ibid.

35 Ibid.

36 Ibid, p. 375.

37 Hiebert, p. 261.

"prophet" with "apostle" in the foundation stage of the church. The foundation period of the early church consisted of the prophets and apostles. These gifts both dealt with revelation, and were vitally important to an infant church that was without a complete Bible. The early church would have been an unguided missile without these two gifts/gifted individuals. The church age apostles and prophets provided authority, guidance, and revelation from God before the canon of Scripture was complete. Today those gifts are no longer needed and have passed away, since we have the 66 books of the Bible.

How does this gift of prophecy relate to the passage under our consideration? In this period before the Word of God was complete, Paul wrote that the Thessalonians were to stop quenching the Holy Spirit in the assembly (v. 19). One area in which they were putting out the flame/stifling the Spirit's work among them when they came together as a church is mentioned in v. 20: "Despise not prophesyings." The word translated "despise" means "to despise someone or something on the basis that it is worthless or of no value."[38] For whatever reason there were some in Thessalonica who were despising the vital gift of prophecy because they believed that it was worthless.

Hiebert does a bit of speculation here that fits the broader context of the book of 1 Thessalonians, and is probably correct:

> More probable is the suggestion of Morris that this despising of prophecy was due to second-advent speculations in the church.[39] From the second epistle (2:3–4) it is clear that, at least a little later, certain self-deceived individuals considered their own speculations on the subject to be the voice of the Spirit. Such abuses of prophecy would naturally cause the more calm and discerning to react against the gift.[40]

---

38 Johannes P. Louw and Eugene Albert Nida, *Greek-English Lexicon of the New Testament: Based on Semantic Domains* (New York: United Bible Societies, 1996), 762.

39 Leon Morris, *The First and Second Epistles to the Thessalonians*, New International Commentary, p. 176.

40 Hiebert, p. 264.

So according to verses 20-21, they were not to despise all prophetic utterances, but neither should they allow the pendulum to swing to the other extreme and accept anything that a prophet, or self-professed prophet said. They were to "prove all things," which means they were to "**make a critical examination of someth[ing]...to determine genuineness, *put to the test, examine*.**"[41] Those who had the spiritual gift of "discerning of spirits" (1 Cor. 12:10) could no doubt be of assistance here. If after examination a prophetic utterance were found to be truly of God, it should be held on to: "hold fast that which is good."

The Verse and Meaning of a Key Word

Keeping in mind what we have seen so far, we now examine the verse in question (1 Thess. 5:22), and the often-confusing translation: "appearance" (KJV). Paul tells the assemblies to "abstain from all appearance of evil." Exactly how does that fit in with his instruction about prophetic utterances? What does it even mean?

First, although in some places in the Greek New Testament, the word translated "appearance" (*eidos*) has the strict meaning of "external appearance" (e.g., Jn. 5:37), it does not here. The well-known, *Thayer's Greek Lexicon* correctly defines it relating to our passage as "*form, kind....,* i. e. from every kind of evil or wrong, 1 Thess. 5:22."[42] [43] Paul

---

41 Frederick William Danker (rev. and ed.). *A Greek-English Lexicon of the New Testament and Other Early Christian Literature, 3rd Edition* (Chicago: The University of Chicago Press, 2000). Entry #2065 δοκιμάζω, BibleWorks, v.10.

42 Joseph Henry Thayer. *A Greek-English Lexicon of the New Testament* (International Bible Translators, Inc., 1998-2000). Entry #1578 εἶδος, BibleWorks, v.10.

43 Leon Morris gives a deeper dive into the use of the word here: "*Eidos* may mean the outward appearance (Luke 3:22, 'form'), or 'sort, species, kind', which appears to be the meaning here. Some think it means 'semblance' (AV 'appearance'), but this sense is not attested and in any case it seems unlikely that Paul would be concerned only with the outward appearance. Our choice seems to be between 'every visible form of evil' (with no notion of unreality) and 'every kind of evil'. The use of the word elsewhere in the New Testament favours the former, but there are enough examples of the term in the latter sense in the papyri...to make it quite possible, and in view of the context, this seems to be the right meaning. Paul is urging his friends to avoid evil of every kind (cf. Rom. 12:9)." (Leon Morris, *1 and 2 Thessalonians: An Introduction and Commentary*, vol. 13, Tyndale New Testament Commentaries (Downers Grove, IL: InterVarsity Press, 1984), 107.)

then was commanding his readers to "abstain/keep away from (Hiebert's literal rendering is "hold yourselves off from."[44]) every form/kind of evil."

Verse 22 forms a contrast to v. 21. Every prophetic utterance should be carefully proven and examined, and as a result, the Thessalonians should hold fast to what is good (true prophetic utterance from the Holy Spirit). On the other side of the coin, they ought to completely abstain/keep away from every form/kind of evil (false prophetic utterance that teaches what is evil). Morris ends with a good thought: "The change from 'the good' (v. 21) to *every kind of evil* may well be significant. The good is one, but evil is manifold; it is to be avoided in all its forms."[45]

The Conclusion

It is clear then that 1 Thessalonians 5:22 is not an injunction to stay away from anything that *appears* to be evil, but was a command to stay away from every *form* of evil false prophetic utterances before the Word of God was complete. Although the gift of prophecy is no longer in operation, the command still has application to us today. We need to judge everything that we hear or read against the complete revelation of God. If what we hear or read does not match up with that book we need to stay away from that evil teaching.

"If we confess our sins, he is faithful and just to forgive us our sins, and to cleanse us from all unrighteousness."
1 John 1:9

Our verse under consideration is often applied incorrectly. Many erroneously use it as a verse to encourage people to place saving faith in Christ as Savior. Their application goes something like this: "If you will come to Jesus by faith and confess your sins, He will forgive you, save you, and cleanse you from all unrighteousness." At first glance the statement may seem harmless, but it not only presents a verse out of context, but it also teaches doctrine that is patently false and unbiblical.

---

44 Hiebert, p. 266.
45 Leon Morris, *1 and 2 Thessalonians: An Introduction and Commentary*, vol. 13, Tyndale New Testament Commentaries (Downers Grove, IL: InterVarsity Press, 1984), 107.

Should those who have never received Christ as Savior be urged to confess their sins in order to be saved? The answer must be an emphatic and resounding "No!" Those who do not know the Lord are never commanded to confess their individual sins, but instead are asked to acknowledge that they are *sinners* (Rom. 3:23).

The Context Makes the Meaning Obvious

To understand the meaning of this text, we must first identify the "we" of 1:9. Keep in mind that when the author uses "we," he is including himself in the statement. Keep in mind that each text of Scripture only has ONE CORRECT MEANING. Biblical texts do not have multiple meanings. Multiple applications are possible, but multiple meanings are not. Without a consideration of the context, as I see it, there are only four possible options to choose from concerning the meaning of "we" in 1 John 1:9: **1)** The word "we" is referring to humanity in general (of whom John is a part); **2)** The word "we" is referring to all **un**believers (of whom John is a part); **3)** The word "we" refers to all those who *profess* to know Christ as Savior (some are saved and some are not. . . of whom John is a part); or **4)** the word "we" is referring to all believers (of whom John is a part).

With very little difficulty we should be able to immediately exclude #2 from our consideration. It would be impossible for the "we" to be referring to those who are unsaved, since John would have to be including himself in this group. This would be absurd. Nevertheless, could the "we" of 1 John 1:9 be speaking of mankind in general (#1), or perhaps just professing Christians (#3)? Absolutely not! The context of the book makes this an impossibility. 1:3 tells us that "truly our fellowship is with the Father, and with his Son Jesus Christ." This would not be an appropriate description for either mankind in general, or for those who just professed Christ and didn't actually know Him. Also, notice the following statements found in 2:1-2: "My little children," and "we have an advocate with the Father," as well as "he is the propitiation for our sins." Once again, these statements would not be appropriate descriptions of either #1 or #3.

The only way to sensibly interpret the "we" of verse 9 is as a reference to all believers (#4).

Additional proof for this can be found as we read a bit further into this epistle. Notice in 2:12-14 that John tells us *directly* that he is addressing *believers*:

> I write unto you, little children, because your sins are forgiven you for his name's sake. I write unto you, fathers, because ye have known him *that is* from the beginning. I write unto you, young men, because ye have overcome the wicked one. I write unto you, little children, because ye have known the Father. I have written unto you, fathers, because ye have known him *that is* from the beginning. I have written unto you, young men, because ye are strong, and the word of God abideth in you, and ye have overcome the wicked one.

Just a few verses later, he indicates yet again that he is writing to those who know the truth: "I have not written unto you because ye know not the truth, but because ye know it, and that no lie is of the truth" (2:21). No, John is not writing to humanity in general, or to the unsaved, or to merely professing Christians. Instead, he is addressing **genuine believers**.

Keeping the context in mind, how then do we understand "confession" as it relates to a believer? First, it is important to understand the meaning of the word.

The *Friberg Greek Lexicon* defines the Greek word *homologeo* ("confess"): "from a basic meaning *say the same thing*. . . as confessing that something is true *admit, agree...of an acknowledgment of sins confess....*"[46] God wants believers, when they sin, to immediately confess/admit/agree with Him about their sin. Continual confession of known sin is an important part of the Christian life. Dr. W. Hall Harris writes in his internet commentary: "...the author points out that if Christians confess the sins they are aware of, they may be sure that God will forgive

---

46 Timothy Friberg, Barbara Friberg, and Neva F. Miller. *Analytical Lexicon to the Greek New Testament* (Grand Rapids: Baker, 2000). Entry #19688 ὁμολογέω, BibleWorks, v.10.

their sins and cleanse them not only from those sins they confess but from *all unrighteousness*."[47]

If this is something that all believers are called upon to do, what is its purpose? Does it help us to retain our salvation? If we fail to do as commanded, does it mean that we lose our salvation? No, 1 John 1:9 has nothing to do with the Christian "keeping his salvation." It is *not* that forgiveness at the point of salvation mentioned in Col. 1:14: "...redemption through his blood, *even* the <u>forgiveness</u> of sins." It is following salvation. It is the forgiveness that a father extends to a son when he has sinned. Moreover, it is not an act that keeps a person "saved." A disobedient son doesn't cease to be a son, but he does affect the intimacy of the relationship with his father when he lives in rebellion. The same is true of the believer.

J. Dwight Pentecost explains the injunction given to believers:

When the believer sins, the blood of Christ is instantaneously, automatically applied to the believer (v. 7), maintaining his sonship with the Father, but sin has broken fellowship. My child may strain our relationship by disobeying, but he is still my child. Disobedience does not affect position, it affects fellowship. To be restored to fellowship with God we must confess our sin."[48]

Donald Burdick explains further:

It must be remembered that this epistle was written to those who already are forgiven (2:12). John is not here speaking of the initial forgiveness of sin which occurs at the point of salvation. At that time the guilt of all one's sins -- past, present and future -- is forgiven. The forgiveness of this verse, however, is an experience which comes after salvation. Its function is to remove that which has disturbed the believer's fellowship with

---

47 W. Hall Harris III. "Exegetical Commentary on 1 John 1:5-2:2," from Bible.Org website: https://bible.org/seriespage/6-exegetical-commentary-1-john-15-22. (Accessed October 12, 2023).

48 J. Dwight Pentecost. *The Joy of Fellowship* (Grand Rapids: Zondervan Publishing House, 1977), pp. 30-31.

God. Whereas the former is a legal remission of guilt, the latter is the Father's forgiveness of His child to restore undisturbed communion."[49]

Zane Hodges concurs with Pentecost and Burdick:

What is considered in 1 John 1:9 may be described as "familial" forgiveness. It is perfectly understandable how a son may need to ask his father to forgive him for his faults while at the same time his position within the family is not in jeopardy. A Christian who never asks his heavenly Father for forgiveness for his sins can hardly have much sensitivity to the ways in which he grieves his Father. Furthermore, the Lord Jesus Himself taught His followers to seek forgiveness of their sins in a prayer that was obviously intended for daily use.... The teaching that a Christian should not ask God for daily forgiveness is an aberration. Moreover, confession of sin is *never* connected by John with the acquisition of eternal life, which is always conditioned on faith. First John 1:9 is not spoken to the unsaved, and the effort to turn it into a soteriological affirmation is misguided.[50]

Concluding Thoughts

How careful we need to be in our application of 1 John 1:9. To the unsaved man, sin is a matter between a lawbreaker and the Judge; but to the believer, sin is a matter between a son and his Father. Confession of sin does not maintain the believer's *salvation*, but it maintains the son's close *fellowship* with his Heavenly Father. 1 John 1:9 encourages believers to daily and continually confess known sin as the Holy Spirit brings it to our minds. 1 John 1:9 should never be used as an encouragement for people to receive Christ as Savior. It is clearly a passage directed only to believers.

---

49 Donald W. Burdick. *The Epistles of John* (Chicago: Moody Press, 1970), pp. 26-27.

50 John F. Walvoord and Roy B. Zuck, Dallas Theological Seminary, *The Bible Knowledge Commentary: An Exposition of the Scriptures*, vol. 2 (Wheaton, IL: Victor Books, 1985), p. 886.

"Behold, I stand at the door, and knock: if any man hear my voice, and open the door, I will come in to him, and will sup with him, and he with me." Rev. 3:20

Revelation 3:20 is a passage that has been used for many years in gospel presentations. It is normally used as a "clincher" verse to demonstrate a person's need for personal acceptance of Christ as Savior from sin. The common narrative that goes along with this passage is something similar to the following: "Christ is knocking at your heart's door right now, and all you must do to be saved is invite Him in." Most picture in their minds Warner Sallman's famous picture, *Christ Knocking at Heart's Door,* but is this an appropriate and contextually accurate way to apply this passage? Furthermore, is this application theologically correct? I believe that the answer to both of these questions must be a resounding "No!"

The context clearly shows that Revelation 3:20 was never intended to be used as a salvation verse at all, but is actually an exhortation to *believers.* I want us to understand the meaning of this verse, first by pointing out the hermeneutical errors of interpreting it as a salvation verse. Second, by using sound hermeneutics, I want to point out the contextually accurate meaning of the passage.

A Defective Interpretation

Is Revelation 3:20 a salvation passage? What does the context show? What does the text say? In Revelation 3, verses 14-22 we find the last of the messages to the seven churches. Verse 14 tells us that Christ is addressing this letter to the "angel[51] of the church of the Laodiceans." From this point on, there is no indication whatsoever that our Lord is dealing with anyone else but believers. No doubt these Christians were disobedient, careless, and complacent, although the context does not even hint to the reader that these people were anything but genuine believers.

---

51 Most assuredly a reference to the pastor of the "mother church," and not a reference to an angelic being.

Verse 19 is clear that the Lord is addressing the Laodiceans as *believers*: "as many as I love." The Greek verb translated "love" here is *phileo*. As Greek scholar, Dr. Daniel B. Wallace writes,

> Here φιλέω is used for "love"--a term that is *never* used of God/Jesus loving unbelievers in the NT. (Indeed, it would be impossible for God to have this kind of love for an unbeliever, for it routinely speaks of enjoyment and fellowship. ἀγαπάω, rather, is the verb used of God's love for unbelievers [cf. John 3:16], for it frequently, if not normally, speaks of commitment and, when used with God/Jesus as the subject, the idea is often of an unconditional love.[52]

Notice too that the passage indicates that those whom Christ loves He disciplines. According to Hebrews 12:6-8, only true sons are disciplined by the Lord, <u>not</u> those who are unsaved:

> For whom the Lord loveth he chasteneth, and scourgeth every son whom he receiveth. If ye endure chastening, God dealeth with you as with sons; for what son is he whom the father chasteneth not? But if ye be without chastisement, whereof all are partakers, then are ye bastards, and not sons.

God *does not* discipline those who are not His. The context reveals that only *saved* people are in view in Revelation 3:20, not unbelievers. Walvoord agrees: "This was an appeal to Christians rather than to non-Christians."[53]

Additionally, the concept of a person "inviting Jesus into his heart" at salvation is also attributed to this verse. It is based upon a careless translation of *eiseleusomai pros auton*. The English versions we have are generally not the problem. The problem is with the interpreter who reads the text incorrectly. The text clearly states, "I will come **in to** him."

---

52 Daniel B. Wallace. *Revelation 3:20 and the Offer of Salvation.* May 25, 2004. https:// bible.org/article/revelation-320-and-offer-salvation (Accessed January 25, 2022).

53 John F. Walvoord, "Revelation," in *The Bible Knowledge Commentary: An Exposition of the Scriptures*, ed. J. F. Walvoord and R. B. Zuck, vol. 2 (Wheaton, IL: Victor Books, 1985), 942.

This is quite different however from the common misunderstanding, "I will come **into** him." The two meanings are quite different.

Neither the Greek nor the English hints at *penetration* ("into" the heart), but rather *direction* ("in to" be with the person). If Christ had been indicating penetration into the human heart, the Greek word *eis* would have been used, and the translation "I will come into him" would be justified. However, the Greek word *pros* is used here, indicating here *motion toward* someone. Wallace clarifies the issue for us:

> The idea of "come into" would be expressed with εἰς as the independent preposition and would suggest a penetration into the person (thus, spawning the idea of entering into one's heart). However, spatially πρός means *toward*, not *into*. In all eight instances of εἰσέρχομαι πρός in the NT, the meaning is "come in toward/before a person" (i.e., enter a building, house, etc., so as to be in the presence of someone), *never penetration* into the person himself/herself. In some instances, such a view would not only be absurd, but inappropriate (cf. Mark 6:25; 15:43; Luke 1:28; Acts 10:3; 11:3;16:40; 17:2; 28:8).[54]

It is best to avoid such expressions as "inviting Jesus into your heart." It is, *at best*, an expression that is extra-biblical and theologically questionable. Moreover, the terminology can create great confusion in the minds of children.[55] It would be far better to use the *Biblical* terms "believe" and "faith."

A Proper Understanding

In Revelation 3:20 Christ is portrayed as standing outside the lives of church members. The Laodicean church had become complacent and self-sufficient. They no longer felt that they needed the Lord, for they were "rich, and increased with goods," and "had need of nothing." They

---

54 Daniel B. Wallace. *Revelation 3:20 and the Offer of Salvation*. May 25, 2004. https://bible.org/article/revelation-320-and-offer-salvation (Accessed October 9, 2023).

55 How well I remember a Junior High student telling me of the time when her little brother "asked Jesus into his stomach" because he couldn't understand how Jesus could live in a person's heart! The young child missed the point.

were about to be judged, and now Christ tenderly appeals to them one more time, as individuals, to return to intimate fellowship with Him.

Warren Wiersbe says of vv. 20-22:

> We often use these verses to lead lost people to Christ, but the basic application is to the believer. The Lord was outside the Laodicean church! He spoke to the individual — "if any man" — and not to the whole congregation. He appealed to a small remnant in Sardis (Rev. 3:4–5), and now He appeals to the individual. God can do great things in a church, even through one dedicated individual.

> Christ was not impatient. "I have taken My stand" is the sense of the verb. He "knocks" through circumstances and He calls through His Word. For what is He appealing? Fellowship and communion, the people's desire to abide in Him. The Laodiceans were an independent church that had need of nothing, but they were not abiding in Christ and drawing their power from Him. They had a "successful program" but it was not fruit that comes from abiding in Christ (John 15:1–8).[56]

Christ's appeal to individuals of the church is to *open the door* ("if any man hear my voice, and open the door") to let Him back into the individual's miserable, empty life. At that point the intimate relationship with his Lord will be restored ("I will come in to him, and will sup with him, and he with me.").

Concerning the word translated "sup/dine" (*deipneso*), it is a metaphor for fellowship. J. Hampton Keathley III writes:

> **"Dine is a Greek word which referred to the main meal of the day** — a real feast. This Greek word, *deipneo*, was used not only of the chief meal of the day — a full course dinner — but of the meal which was the occasion for hospitality and fellowship. At this meal, however, He is the host. It is He who

---

56 Warren W. Wiersbe, *The Bible Exposition Commentary*, vol. 2 (Wheaton, IL: Victor Books, 1996), 581.

sets the table and we are His guests dining on that which He has provided."[57]

Revelation 3:20 is clearly a passage written to Christians to repent of sin and be restored to full fellowship with the Lord. Keathley agrees, "Actually, this passage is addressed to the church—to believers. This is a call to fellowship with the Savior. As an invitation to Christians, it's a call to repent, as commanded in verse 19. It is a call for confession of one's sins with a renewal of mind and heart to continue to draw upon the glorious life of Christ daily through walking by the Spirit and living in the Word. It means abiding in Christ, the vine (John 15:1-7; 1 John 1:7-10; Eph. 4:20-24; 5:14-18; Rom. 8:1-16)."[58]

We who know Christ ought to use great care in giving out the gospel, making sure that our terminology is Biblical, and that we are accurately communicating the meaning of the passages that we relate to the lost. If we are guilty of using a text inaccurately just because it "fits" into our gospel presentation, how much different are we really from the cults who pervert Biblical texts to fit into their twisted message?

---

57 J. Hampton III Keathley, *Studies in Revelation: Christ's Victory over the Forces of Darkness* (Biblical Studies Press, 1997), p. 84.

58 Ibid.

CONCLUSION

As we seek to "get it right" and apply the principles of Biblical interpretation that we have learned in this book, there are several personal things that are vital to remember.

Salvation Comes First

An unsaved person can be skilled at language and grammatical analysis, but only those who know Jesus Christ as Savior have the ability to truly *understand* God's Word (1 Cor. 2:14). The Lord Jesus died, was buried, and rose again to pay the penalty for your sin (1 Cor. 15:3-4). If you have never been born again through faith alone in Christ alone, won't you trust Him as your Savior from sin right now?

The Assistance of the Holy Spirit Is Vital

Although study and accurate interpretation are important, they aren't everything. We must walk with, be filled with, and depend on the Holy Spirit in our studies and ministry (Eph. 5:18).

Don't Be Discouraged That You Don't Have the Skill and Knowledge of Some

Do the best that you can with the maturity and knowledge that God has given you. You may not have all of the knowledge and tools to study the Bible as some people do, but if you know Christ, you do have the same Great Teacher (John 14:26) living inside of you!

We All Fail at Times in Interpreting the Word of God

Keep in mind that as diligent and sincere as we may be in following a normal hermeneutic, at times we all still struggle with applying the principles of Biblical interpretation. No matter how skilled we are, we are still fallible, and will sometimes come to the wrong conclusions about a text.

I've been in the ministry just shy of 40 years, and there have been times when I have failed miserably in accurately interpreting the Bible. Perhaps I taught one thing for several years, and then later discovered that what I had been teaching was wrong. As a perfectionist and hard-working student of God's Word, when I fall flat in interpreting a text incorrectly it bothers me profoundly, particularly if I have preached/taught it to others. If I'm not watchful, my natural tendency is to grovel in self-deprecation. This is pride and sin.

Learn from my weakness. When you make a mistake in interpretation, correct it with those whom you have taught, and move on. Not that we ought to be complacent toward our failures, but we should not wallow in self-pity either. We need to be grateful to God for the ability that He has given us to study and determine the meaning of the text. We are all learning and growing.

Learn to Properly Use the Thoughts of Others

Bob Jones, Sr. used to say, "You can borrow wisdom, but you can't borrow character." It's alright in your studies to use tools such as commentaries, and to "borrow other's wisdom." However, make sure that you are evaluating the text by yourself *first* and allowing the Great Teacher to help you understand it. Afterwards, check yourself by digging into the commentaries. Don't just take what others say as "gospel." Be a faithful and diligent student of God's Word.

Pray Before You Study

Pray before you begin studying God's Word! Ask for God's help in properly interpreting it. Pray that the Holy Spirit will teach you as you study.

My father told the story of a man whom someone discovered had the word "pray" written at the top of *every page* of his Bible! Puzzled, the person asked him why he had done that. He responded that he wrote the word "pray" repetitively so that whatever passage he turned to he would be reminded to pray and ask for God's guidance and help before he studied God's Word. We would do well to remind ourselves to do the same!

Collect Basic Tools for Study

Purchase a study Bible (the *Ryrie Study Bible* is my favorite), and a basic library of study tools and commentaries. It's beyond the scope of this book to detail how to assemble a personal library, but there are several books available on the subject of Bible study that have a chapter or section that lists a basic set of books that every believer ought to have. Computer tools will also save money and space.

Finally...

We are stewards of the Word of God. As such we need to be faithful to this precious trust from the Lord and handle His Book carefully. As stewards, accuracy and precision are vitally important because "getting it right" has eternal implications not only for us (2 Cor. 5:10), but also for those to whom we minister.

SELECTED BIBLIOGRAPHY

Fruchtenbaum, Arnold G. *Israelology: The Missing Link in Systematic Theology*, Rev. ed. Tustin, CA: Ariel Ministries, 1994.

Hoyt, Herman A. Expository Messages on the New Birth. Grand Rapids: Baker Book House, 1961.

Hoyt, Samuel L. *The Judgment Seat of Christ: A Biblical and Theological Study*, Rev. Ed. Duluth, MN: Grace Gospel Press, 2021.

Makujina, John. *Measuring the Music: Another Look at the Contemporary Christian Music Debate*, 3rd Ed. Fort Worth, TX: Religious Affections Ministries, 2016.

Nuttall, Clayton L. *The Weeping Church: Confronting the Crisis of Church Polity.* Schaumburg, IL: Regular Baptist Press, 1985.

Nuttall, Clay L. and Hanna, Hani. *The Normal Hermeneutic: The Only Biblical Hermeneutic.* North Fort Myers, FL: Faithful Life Publishers, 2018.

Pentecost, J. Dwight. *The Words and Works of Jesus Christ: A Study of the Life of Christ.* Grand Rapids, Zondervan Publishing House, 1981.

___. *Things to Come.* Grand Rapids: Zondervan, 1958.

___. *Thy Kingdom Come: Tracing God's Kingdom Program and Covenant Promises Throughout History.* Grand Rapids: Kregel Publications, 1995.

Ryrie, Charles Caldwell. *A Survey of Bible Doctrine.* Chicago: Moody Press, 1972.

___. *Basic Theology: A Popular Systematic Guide to Understanding Biblical Truth.* Chicago, IL: Moody Press, 1999.

___. *Dispensationalism*, Rev. and expanded. Chicago: Moody Publishers, 1995.

___. *Ryrie's Practical Guide to Communicating Bible Doctrine*. Nashville, TN: Broadman & Holman Publishers, 2005.

___. *Ryrie Study Bible, 1995 Update*, Expanded ed. Chicago: Moody Press, 1995.

Showers, Renald E. *The Most High God: Commentary on the Book of Daniel*. Bellmawr, NJ: FOI Gospel Ministry, Inc., 1982.

___. *There Really Is a Difference!: A Comparison of Covenant and Dispensational Theology*. Bellmawr, NJ: FOI Gospel Ministry, Inc., 1990.

Tan, Paul Lee. *Literal Interpretation of the Bible*. Rockville, MD: Assurance Publishers, 1978.

Wood, Leon J. *Daniel*. Grand Rapids, MI: Zondervan Publishing House, 1975.

Woods, Andy. *Ever Reforming: Dispensational Theology and the Completion of the Protestant Reformation*. Taos, NM: Dispensational Publishing House, 2018.

Zuck, Roy B. *Basic Bible Interpretation: A Practical Guide to Discovering Biblical Truth*. Edited by Craig Bubeck Sr. Colorado Springs, CO: David C. Cook, 1991.

ABOUT THE AUTHOR

Dr. Bob Payne was born in Detroit, Michigan, the youngest of four children. He accepted Christ as Savior when he was 12 years old.

He attended Bob Jones University in Greenville, South Carolina, and completed his Bachelor's degree at Faith Baptist Bible College in Ankeny, Iowa. He also earned a Th.M. and Th.D. (*summa cum laude*) from Andersonville Theological Seminary in Camilla, Georgia. He received further graduate training at International Baptist Seminary in Chandler, AZ.

Dr. Payne has taught various Biblical and theological subjects at the college and graduate level in the United States, the Middle East, North Africa, and Canada. For many years he was an adjunct faculty member at the National Theological College and Graduate School based in Lexington, NC, and is presently a visiting faculty member at the Biblical Theological Seminary in Amman, Jordan.

With 37 years of experience in the ministry, Dr. Bob Payne has dedicated his life to shepherding God's people. He has served as a pastor in various locations, including Nebraska, Michigan, New Brunswick (Canada), and Connecticut. Since 2017, he has been the pastor of the historic Baptist Church of Danbury, Connecticut. He has also been the moderator and an officer in the Independent Baptist Fellowship of North America (IBFNA).

Dr. Payne has been married for 37 years and has a daughter and three grandchildren.

Printed in the USA
CPSIA information can be obtained
at www.ICGtesting.com
LVHW051126281023
762442LV00011B/903